Praise for *Forgive Your Way to Freedom*

Forgiveness is a core tenet of the Christian life, but it's also one of the most difficult biblical commands to put into practice! In this thoughtful and inspiring work, Gil Mertz shows us how forgiveness doesn't just benefit those on the receiving end—it also brings *us* into greater joy and freedom.

JIM DALY
President—Focus on the Family

Gil has identified the most important quality to cling to and to release, forgiveness. Clinging to our own forgiveness through Christ empowers us to release others from being captive to our internal prisons. This is a must-read to understand true freedom.

TAMMY DUNAHOO
General Supervisor and Vice-President of US Operations, Foursquare Church

There is no doubt that the issue and the need for forgiveness is paramount to any healthy and meaningful relationship. Far too many people have misunderstood what it means to truly forgive and to be forgiven. In his well-written book, Gil Mertz sets forth the simple truth that receiving God's forgiveness for yourself and extending that forgiveness to others literally sets you free to live more like Jesus Christ. This wonderful book will enable you to be that agent of change for healing and hope.

JACK HIBBS
Senior Pastor, Calvary Chapel Chino Hills, California

I've spent most of my career in Washington, D.C., which is one of the places in America where forgiveness is most needed. I encourage you to get a copy of this practical and helpful book for yourself. You may also want to share a copy with someone you know who needs this message (even, perhaps, with one of your elected representatives). You will both be better off for it.

WILLIAM BENNETT, PhD, JD
Former Secretary of Education, host of The Bill Bennett Podcast, and *NY Times* bestselling author of *The Book of Virtues*

One of my great passions is sharing with audiences about the true liberating power of forgiveness. That's why I'm delighted to recommend *Forgive Your Way to Freedom*. Forgiveness is such a divine blessing and the biblical truths that Gil brings out are profound, but the steps and tools he provides are so simple. Gil's book is for anyone who needs to give or receive forgiveness. If you or someone you love wants to experience the power and freedom of forgiveness, I highly recommend you check out this book. It's full of truth that can set you free.

AL ROBERTSON
Star of A&E's Duck Dynasty, pastor, speaker, and author

Forgiveness is one of the most important things in our lives and yet it's also one of the most misunderstood. Gil not only makes a powerful case for forgiveness, but he also shows you how. If you or someone you love is ready to be set free from the shackles of your painful past to embrace a new future with purpose, I encourage you to read *Forgive Your Way to Freedom* and pass it on.

MIKE HUCKABEE
Politician, bestselling author, and host of the "Huckabee" TV show

As a survivor of abuse, I understand all too well how difficult it can be to forgive. I also understand the power and freedom that comes when we can lay down our bitterness and anger and truly embrace forgiveness. Gil Mertz articulates the power of forgiveness so beautifully in this vulnerable and compelling book. It speaks to all of us.

JOHANNA TROPIANO
Executive Director, The Mend Project

I am so glad to see Gil Mertz's beautifully written book *Forgive Your Way to Freedom*. An important step to recovery is empowering people who thought they were powerless. The many tools in this book give the reader the rare opportunity—the gift—of taking their power back. Gil's book is loaded with powerful stories, quotes, and techniques that help the reader find the path to the darkness in his or her heart and letting the sunshine in. This is truly healing stuff!

DAN STRADFORD
Founder and President of Safe Harbor, home of AlternativeMentalHealth.com

I've known Gil for many years and I appreciate his heart for forgiveness, which he has poured into *Forgive Your Way to Freedom*. This is such an important topic in our world that seems to be growing more divided and cynical every day. I believe this book will not only help people find freedom from their past hurts, but it will also help people develop a lifestyle of forgiveness to give them peace and purpose in their daily lives.

MICHELE BACHMANN
Former congresswoman and presidential candidate

Gil Mertz is a man of grace. He is also a man of forgiveness. Forgiveness is something we all need to give and receive. Gil shows us in this wonderful book how true forgiveness can transform us and free us to become the person God wants us to be. If you want to truly live . . . learn to forgive. If you want to forgive your way to freedom, read this book!

CHARLES BILLINGSLEY
Gospel Recording Artist and Author of *Words on Worship*

Most Christians know they should forgive, but when was the last time you can remember being taught how to forgive? Gil Mertz provides just such a road map filled with practical advice on the process of forgiving. This book is a must-read if you want to discover freedom from life's difficult moments that only forgiveness can bring.

DICK TIBBITS, DMIN
Author of *Forgive to Live*

A common mistake travelers make is carrying excess baggage. Unnecessary suitcases not only cost you at the check-in counter, but they wear you out as you carry them around. The same is true with injured relationships. In this practical book, Gil Mertz not only points out the high cost of unforgiveness, but how we can leave the baggage of past hurts behind. If you want to travel through life with a spring in your step, this is the book for you!

J. KENT EDWARDS, PHD, DMIN
Professor of Preaching & Leadership at Talbot School of Theology and BIOLA University

When we think of forgiveness, we often focus too much on the challenges and not enough on the benefits. This is what I appreciate so much about *Forgive Your Way to Freedom*. Gil helps guide the reader through the journey with practical steps that anyone can do, but he also illustrates the reward at the end, which is freedom. When we are empowered by freedom, there is no limit to what we can do!

STAR PARKER
Author and President of the Center for Urban Renewal and Education (CURE)

Gil Mertz is one of my favorite human beings on the planet. He's a gifted communicator and a brilliant writer. *Forgive Your Way to Freedom* helps us navigate our way to a full life in Christ. But to be set free, we have to be willing to forgive—and Gil shows us the path.

TODD STARNES
TV commentator and radio host on Fox News Radio

There are few issues today that impact our lives more than forgiveness. The challenge is not if we should forgive but understanding how to forgive, which Gil Mertz addresses so powerfully in *Forgive Your Way to Freedom*. The practical steps that are clearly outlined in this book can help anyone who is struggling to forgive find the peace, joy, and freedom they need. Well done, Gil! I highly recommend this book!

RICH BOTT
President/CEO of the Bott Radio Network

When the church leads the way by embracing the power of love and forgiveness between us and God and one another, we will see revival in America like we have never seen before. We are One Blood / One Human Race who can learn to live together as brothers and sisters and not perish together as fools. I'm so encouraged to see this book by Gil Mertz, *Forgive Your Way to Freedom*. If ever we needed a message on forgiveness, it is now. The tools and principles from this book will have a powerful impact.

DR. ALVEDA KING, EVANGELIST
Civil Rights for the Unborn

It is my pleasure to recommend the book *Forgive Your Way to Freedom* by my friend Gil Mertz. In my travels over the years I have seen the ravages of war between nations, but I've also seen the personal war of the soul when people cannot forgive. I'm a big believer in freedom, and Gil's book offers hope and help to anyone who is looking to be set free through the power of forgiveness.

LTCOL OLIVER NORTH, USMC (RET.)

As long as we live with the human condition of sin, we will need to practice the virtue of forgiving others and ourselves, and accepting forgiveness. Gil Mertz's book *Forgive Your Way to Freedom* serves as a refreshing and much-needed guide in a hurting world about how we can change our lives and the lives of those around us by tapping into the transformative power and freedom of forgiveness.

ARINA O. GROSSU
Board Member, National Catholic Prayer Breakfast

forgive your way to freedom

Reconcile Your Past
and Reclaim Your Future

GIL MERTZ

MOODY PUBLISHERS
CHICAGO

To the two most important women in my life:

My mother, Katherine.
My angel and my hero.

My wife, Patricia.
Your precious love brought us together.
Your enduring forgiveness keeps us together.

Contents

Foreword

The national surveys I conduct consistently show that most people believe they have been significantly harmed or intentionally taken advantage of by our social institutions, our public leaders, by family members and friends. It seems as if everyone is pointing an accusing finger at someone else for the problems that beset us. We have become divided, angry, distrustful, skeptical, and self-protecting.

The necessary antidote is forgiveness.

God sent His Son to earth in order to reconcile us to Himself —a holy, righteous, perfect, omnipotent, omniscient deity who created us for His purposes. God could easily have wiped out humanity and replaced us with a new set of creatures to bring Him joy and pleasure – but He didn't. Instead, He demonstrated a choice and behavior that should characterize our life: forgiveness.

Jesus Christ's death on a cross saved us—though we have committed offenses that deserve punishment—from permanent pain and suffering. His death was about providing God's ultimate love—forgiveness for our willful disobedience to Him. That gift is often called grace or mercy, but it is also a genuine miracle.

Forgiveness produces miracles of reconciliation and love, day in and day out.

So, Jesus modeled forgiveness for us. And now we live in an era when forgiveness may be the one thing that can save us. It will not be easy for us to embrace a lifestyle of forgiveness because each of us must participate in constant acts of grace-giving. The

Bible exhorts us to forgive others – not just seven times, as the apostle Peter was hoping, but an unlimited number of times, according to Jesus (Matt. 18:21–35; Luke 17:3). But other passages describe our obligation related to forgiveness: to forgive anyone who offends us (Matt. 6:12–15; Mark 11:25; Luke 6:37; Col. 3:13), to ask others for forgiveness (1 Sam. 25:28; Dan. 9:19; 2 Cor. 12:13), to revel in the joy of forgiving or being forgiven (Ps. 32:1).

Perhaps our lethargic response to God's forgiveness of our sins is related to the fact that so many of us take our salvation through God's grace for granted, forgetting how special His love and forgiveness toward us is.

Perhaps it is because so few of us regularly study the Bible to better understand how He calls us to live, and the "best practices" that bring joy and fulfillment into our lives.

Maybe it is because love has become a feeling instead of a way of life in which forgiveness is a necessary and irreplaceable act of proof that we love someone (Prov. 17:9; Num. 14:19; Ps. 86:5).

Or it could be that we minimize the importance of forgiveness because we simply do not believe that the failure to regularly forgive others is a sin, much less a reflection of the state of our heart and mind, or that God is even aware of our willingness to forgive those who offend us.

The end result is that our faith, relationships, communities, governments, and lifestyles are defiled by our failure to forgive. The ramification is that we become unable to live together because we lack the ability to love each other. You can only love others when you offer them the grace and mercy extended through genuine forgiveness.

In spite of calls for greater understanding and unity in our world, my research consistently shows that most of us expect others to give ground in order to produce that cohesion. Waiting for others to change, rather than personally embracing the needed change, rarely produces the desired results. The responsibility to take the first step is on our shoulders, and forgiveness of those who have hurt us or offended us is a necessary first step toward healing.

Remember, choices have consequences. Our choice of whether or not to forgive others, as God has freely forgiven us, generates serious consequences for our life and our world. It is time for us to earnestly and humbly ask for and offer forgiveness to those in our midst.

Toward that end, it is my prayer that Gil Mertz's words on the pages that follow will help us all to grasp and model forgiveness, both for our collective and individual well-being.

GEORGE BARNA
Ventura, California
May 2018

How Good a Forgiver Are You?

The concept of forgiveness is as universal as the law of gravity. It applies to everyone. Every religion encourages and practices it, and even among those who claim no religion at all, forgiveness has an appeal. However, forgiveness is clearly the centerpiece of the Christian faith, which is the basis for this book. Over my more than forty years of ministry, I have observed three common responses from people when they are confronted with a teaching about forgiveness. They are complacent, convicted, or confused.

Complacency says: "I know everything I need to know about forgiveness."

Perhaps this is true, but I'm certain this teaching will take you down new paths you've not discovered about forgiving and being forgiven. I urge you to approach this book with an open mind and a soft heart like the psalmist David who said, "Search me, God, and know my heart; test me and know my anxious thoughts. See if there is any offensive way in me, and lead me in the way everlasting" (Ps. 139:23–24).

Conviction says: "I know everything I want to know about forgiveness."

This is an uncomfortable subject for some because it represents unfinished business in their life that they'd rather not deal with, so they push it away. This book is not about guilt that is hard and cuts. It's about grace that is soft and heals.

Confusion says: "I have no idea what I need or want about forgiveness."

According to polling data from the Barna Group, many people, including Christians, do not understand what the Bible teaches about forgiveness. Look at these statistics:

54 percent of the population believes that unforgiveness is not a sin.

55 percent believe there are no consequences for not forgiving or showing mercy.

54 percent believe they would need to stop feeling angry in order to forgive.

42 percent do not believe they must always forgive.[1]

If these numbers are true, what percent of the population *are practicing forgiveness?*

Forgiveness is not a singular action but a process. Forgiveness is not the destination but the means to get us there. The ultimate goal and reward of forgiveness is freedom. Freedom from our hurtful pasts that can hold us back. Freedom to live out our daily lives in peace and victory. Freedom to pursue our future with purpose and hope. Though we may know we're supposed to forgive, we need someone to show us how. This book will show you how to forgive your way to freedom.

Before you get started, I've prepared a Forgiveness Evaluation of twenty-five questions, which you'll find in Appendix A on page 193, to help you determine where you might be in the forgiveness process. You may think you've got it down pat. Or you may think you aren't as good at it as you actually are. So you'll want to take the evaluation to get a more honest and objective view. Once you discover your results and have a benchmark, this book will really come alive as you can relate each teaching to your own situation.

You'll take this evaluation again once you've finished working your way through the book to see how far you've come to forgiving your way to freedom.

Be sure to answer each question honestly! The more honest and open you are with yourself, the stronger your experience will be as you journey through this process. And be encouraged: Jesus told us that it is the truth that sets us free.[2]

Part 1

UNDERSTAND
FORGIVENESS—
UNLEASH
YOUR POWER

CHAPTER 1

The Power to Set You Free

*"To forgive is to set a prisoner free
and discover that the prisoner was you."*

Lewis B. Smedes

F orgiveness is one of those rare subjects that affects every person, every relationship, every marriage, every family, every one of us.

Whenever I teach on forgiveness to any size crowd, I often start by asking two simple questions:

1. Have you ever been hurt by someone you needed to forgive?
2. Have you ever hurt someone and needed to seek their forgiveness?

If you answered yes to either of those questions, this book is for you.

When I refer to forgiveness, it's not so much about forgiving the rude person who took your place in line at the store, the guy who cut you off on the freeway, or the inconsiderate couple who talked too loud at the theater while you were trying to watch a movie. That's more about extending common grace that we all need, because let's be honest, sometimes that person is us.

But all of us have experienced some level of offense or personal violation that requires more than just common grace. Often these painful experiences are so personal, so hurtful, and so grievous that they tattoo themselves on our hearts and leave indelible scars on our souls. If left unresolved, they ingrain themselves into every fabric of our lives and affect the way we think, how we feel, what we choose to believe as true, and ultimately how we live every day.

Unfortunately this often leads to more sorrow than was perpetrated on us when the offense first occurred. It impacts our quality of life, how we feel about ourselves, our choices, our work, our relationships, our marriage, our children, our family, and future generations. So much of the misery we needlessly carry offers nothing but dysfunction and heartache. And no amount of denial or avoidance can heal our hearts or give us the freedom we desire.

The antidote is forgiveness. To experience life to its fullest, extending and receiving forgiveness must be an ongoing practice for our spiritual, emotional, mental, and physical well-being. Since none of us is perfect, simply put, there is nothing we need *more than forgiveness.*

How do I know this is true?

Though I've done an enormous amount of study on the subject, most of what I know about forgiveness is not based on abstract theories or lessons I've learned in a classroom. Since 1976 I have been involved in full-time Christian ministry, and during that time I have seen the miraculous transformation that happens when people forgive. I have also seen the terrible devastation when people refuse to forgive. But my passion for helping people forgive their way to freedom has been most shaped by my own experiences.

A Deep Wound Healed

One afternoon in the early spring of 2002, I received a phone call from my oldest sister, Sue. She was calling to tell me our dad was dying. He had been fighting cancer for the past year, and it now appeared his days were numbered. At the time, I was living in Los Angeles, almost two thousand miles away from St. Louis, where my dad lived. She wanted to know if I would make the trip back home for Dad's funeral.

After a short pause I calmly replied, "What would be the point?"

There was no bitterness or anger coloring my response, just indifference. I didn't have a relationship with my dad, and we hadn't spoken for more than a decade. I was just thirteen when he and my mother divorced, after nearly twenty-five years of a difficult marriage. While his departure from our home was sad, it also brought relief from the constant rage and tension that had become unbearable. Our home was already broken; this just made it official.

I had tried to give my dad a lot of grace over the years and believed he was doing the best he knew how. Raising eleven children—I was number seven—on a maintenance man's salary in a twelve-hundred-square-foot house would test the soul of any man. I'm sure many of the mistakes he made in raising his children were modeled for him by his own father, whom I never knew but of whom I heard tales that he was given to fits of rage, abuse, and violence, and likely went back several generations. However, I also believe that each of us can choose whether to break away from our painful pasts or to continue the cycle of abuse, rejection, and abandonment. As for Dad, let me just say he did not choose well.

My relationship with my dad was shaped almost entirely by fear. When he wasn't angry, he made it clear he had little interest in our daily lives. As a child, I reasoned that my siblings and I must be really bad kids to have a dad so angry, disappointed, and disengaged.

The one anomaly was when he took me to a St. Louis Cardinals game with some free tickets he got from work. During the bus ride, he told me stories of his service as a medic in training during World War II, which I had never heard before. And as we crossed the busy street, he actually held my hand, the one and only time he ever did. All the sights, sounds, and smells of this experience—even the taste of the soda pop—are still etched in my mind. For one memorable evening, I got to experience what normal felt like with my dad.

Ten years had passed since then, and he was about to die. And I didn't care.

I played football throughout high school, but my dad never saw a game. At one game, I scored the winning touchdown as the clock ran out, and as all the other players' fathers were cheering for me, I wished my own dad had been there to see it. He didn't come to my high school graduation, and on my wedding day, he called to say he had to work and wouldn't make it. As I began raising my own family, I drifted from my father completely.

I experienced occasional reminders of this loss, especially when I saw a father and son close together. Men's spiritual retreats or large rallies were always tough for me since it seemed speaker after speaker raved about the godly heritage of their saintly fathers. Sometimes I resented this. *That's nice for you,* I thought, *but what about the rest of us?* I knew lots of men like me must struggle in life in large part because of their dysfunctional dads.

Choosing a card for Father's Day was an annual challenge. Usually I found a blank card and wrote a personal note. However, one Father's Day I decided to go all out. I created and framed a small poster entitled, "Seven Treasures I Learned from My

Father," which highlighted qualities such as honesty, integrity, strong work ethic, morality, and other important lessons. I sent it to my dad, but never heard back from him. I wasn't even sure if he got it. That was the last time I tried reaching out to him.

Ten years had passed since then, and he was about to die. And I didn't care.

I still held deep pain in my heart that hadn't healed, but I was prepared to manage with the tough scabs that had grown over my wounds. As much as I would have loved to reconcile with my dad, it seemed impossible. The last thing I wanted was to reopen those wounds by going to see him before he died, only to have it turn out badly. Besides, I couldn't imagine what I would say in my final words to him. "I love you"? "Thanks for being my dad"? Everything I could say seemed disingenuous.

I decided to let him die without talking to him, and I was okay with that. But over the next few days, God convicted me that I was making the wrong choice. As this conviction grew, I told God I would see my dad on three conditions. I believed these things were impossible, so I felt confident I'd be off the hook.

First, I wanted my grown son, Jamie, to accompany me. Since he lived four hours away from his grandfather and barely knew him, I assumed he would have no interest in making the trip.

Second, I told God I wanted to look my dad in the eye and tell him I forgave him. However, I was sure this would make my dad defensive, and our final meeting would not go well.

Third, I wanted my father to look me in the eye and tell me he loved me. Since he had never done this, I had no expectation that he would do it on his deathbed.

I felt safe making this bargain with God, so I asked my son if he wanted to go with me. I was certain he'd decline, and then I wouldn't have to go. My heart sank when he jumped at the chance. I was moving toward the point of no return, and a little more than a month later I flew to St. Louis.

The night before my visit, I decided to call my dad to let him know I wanted to see him. This call would break more than ten years of silence, and I found myself wondering how he would respond. Would he take my call? Would he agree to a visit? What would I say to him?

"Hello?" His voice sounded weak.

"Hi, Dad. This is Gilbert." (I'm still Gilbert when I'm in trouble or when I visit home.)

"Yeah."

His cool reception threw me off, but I continued. "Well, Dad, I'm in Missouri, and Jamie and I would like to come and see you tomorrow. Would that be okay?"

"Sure, if you want to come."

"Yes, we'd like to come. When can we see you?"

"I have to go to therapy at eleven thirty. Why don't you come at ten thirty?"

I was taken aback by his suggestion. One hour? I hadn't seen him in more than ten years, and he was suggesting that we visit for just an hour? "How about if we come at ten o'clock to give us a little more time to visit?" I said, fighting back my disappointment.

"Well, that's up to you."

"Okay, we'll see you tomorrow morning at ten."

"Okay then, see you tomorrow."

I hung up, feeling hurt and let down by my dad's reaction. "I knew this would happen," I told God angrily. "I knew if I opened my heart and took this chance, I would be disappointed. Why would I want to go see him if he doesn't care to see me? It's such a waste!" My anger soon turned to self-pity, and a flood of tears escaped from me. "Why is it so hard for my father to love me?"

In the darkness of my room as the tears and pain flowed out of me, God drew near to comfort me, and I thought of an unmistakable truth from Psalm 27:10: "Though my father and mother forsake me, the LORD will receive me." God sweetly reminded me that He is my Father and that He loves me with all His being. My anger and fear were soon replaced with an incredible peace, and I fell into the deepest sleep I'd had in a long time.

Early the next morning, Jamie arrived and we headed to see my dad. I felt thankful to have my son with me, but still my heart was pounding. Before we entered the facility, I called my wife, Patricia, and asked her to pray for me.

It was time to see Dad for our last meeting. As we approached the front door, my son put his hand on my shoulder and asked if I was okay.

"No, I'm not okay," I told him. "I'm terrified because I don't know how this is all going to play out. But I want you to know something, Son. There's no one in the world I'd rather have going in there with me than you." With that, we walked arm-in-arm through the door.

My dad's roommate greeted us. He smiled a big toothless grin and said, "You must be Gilbert!" Then he gestured toward a wheelchair and like a game show host, announced, "*Heeeeere's your dad!*"

And there he was. The only man I have ever feared was frail, sitting in a wheelchair. My father certainly didn't look scary now. He was weak, helpless, and too thin. He was so different from the big, strong man with the booming voice I had remembered as a child. I dutifully walked over and gave him a hug, as did Jamie. We then wheeled him into a crowded reception room where we sat and engaged in small talk.

Our conversation was slow and awkward at first. I wondered how we would transition to the kind of serious talk I wanted to have as I realized our visiting time was going by quickly. Since we obviously couldn't have a meaningful exchange in this crowded area, I asked my dad if we could go back to his room.

As we got settled in his room, I took the time to look around. All that was left of his life were some old clothes, a few pairs of shoes, and some Southern Gospel CDs. On the wall, to the right of his bed, hung his most prized possessions: a photo of his daughters and one of his sons. Then my eyes landed on something familiar. Next to the pictures hung an old framed poster that read "Seven Treasures I Learned from My Father."

I felt conflicted. I was glad he had not only received the poster I made for him, but obviously he cherished it. But I also felt sad and confused. *Why didn't he ever tell me he got it?* I wondered. *Why am I just now discovering how much it meant to him, as he's about to die?*

Jamie sat on the bed while I pulled up a chair in front of my dad's wheelchair. To my surprise, Dad appeared to cower as I stood over him. I was now the big man. I was the one in control. He must have dreaded whatever he thought was coming, misinterpreting my strong look of resolve. But when I sat down, tears began to flow down my cheeks.

I took his big hands, which had been instruments of remarkable genius and devastating pain, and kissed them gently. I placed his hands on my face so he could feel my tears. After a few moments of silence, I took a deep breath and said, "After today I'm never going to see you again."

He paused at the weight of that statement, then said, "If what the doctors are telling me is true, then yes, this will be our last visit."

Unsure where to start, I finally asked, "Dad, what do you think of me?"

Another pause. "Well . . . I think highly of all my children. There's Sue, Virginia, Jim—"

"No, I didn't ask what you thought of all your children. I want to know what you think of me, Gilbert."

Again he paused. "Uh . . . I know you're a hard worker. And I know you've been in the ministry a long time." He smiled as if he hoped he had passed the test and this would be enough to satisfy me.

"I didn't ask you about what I've done. I want to know what you think of me."

His face tightened, as though he was stumped, and he sat back in his wheelchair without responding.

I swallowed hard and prayed for boldness. "Dad, last week I turned forty-five years old, and I've never once heard you say you love me."

He looked down as I let him digest that statement. He cleared his throat and said, "You know, my dad never told me he loved me. In fact, it wasn't until the last week of her life that my mother said she loved me."

I looked him in the eyes and said simply, "I forgive you, Dad."

Once again I felt conflicted. How terribly sad that my father would go through life without hearing his parents say they loved him. I felt genuine compassion, yet I also felt resentment. *Because you didn't get it, I don't get it either?* I thought. *Not getting it is no excuse for not giving it.* But I kept these thoughts to myself and instead said, "Dad, because I never heard you say you love me, I have struggled so much in my life. I concluded I was not loveable."

He leaned forward slightly and groaned. I knew this was painful for both of us. He put his frail hands on my cheeks and wiped away my tears, but I still had more to say.

"I've had many people say kind things about me throughout my life, but no one's approval means more to me than yours." This was the most honest and transparent I had ever been with my dad.

He looked down at his lap, as though moved by what I had just said. "Son, I realize I have failed you as a father. Looking back, I wish I had done things differently—"

That was all I needed to hear. I interrupted him again, gently this time, and said something I had thought would be impossible, words I had waited forty-five years to say. I looked him in the eyes and said simply, "I forgive you, Dad."

And I felt free. Truly free for the first time.

My dad wasn't defensive. He wasn't upset. With that simple pronouncement, he was set free too.

Then he looked up, looked me in the eyes, and told me what I had waited forty-five years to hear: "I love you, Son."

We immediately embraced and began to weep. Jamie stood and put his arms around both of us as we all wept together. This scene signified something far more profound than three men hugging and crying. This was the moment a father, son, and grandson together broke a generational curse that had hung over our family for far too long.

I don't remember how long we embraced or what else we said. But there was such a tremendous sense of victory in that room. God had done the impossible—just as He had promised. For me, this would be a watershed event, forever resolving so much inner conflict and pain, and I knew I could now leave my dad in peace.

As we said our final goodbyes, I was struck by the bittersweet sight of my son talking and laughing with his grandpa. Bitter because of all the wasted time and lost opportunities with my dad. But also remarkably sweet because this was one moment we did not let escape. I knew I would always remember this experience.

I held out my hand to him. "Goodbye, Dad."

He took my hand and pulled me close to him so he could look in my face. He gently smiled. "Always remember that I love you."

I kissed him on the head. "I promise, I will never forget."

Outside, I leaned against a fence and cried harder than I had in many years. Jamie came over to me and we held each other in a long embrace.

"Dad, I know you love me."

I didn't expect those words, and I stepped back and put my hands on his shoulders. "Do you, Son? Do you know how much I love you?"

"Of course I do," he said. "I've always known you love me."

"Jamie, you just heard your grandfather say that his dad never told him that he loved him. And probably your great-grandfather's dad made the same mistake. This generational curse ends here and now with you and me! Promise me that when you have your own children, you will tell them over and over how much they are loved."

He promised. What an amazing, healing journey. My dad succumbed to his cancer shortly after our visit. I have never forgotten his final words to me, and I

The reason forgiveness has so much power is because when we forgive, we are most like God!

repeat them constantly to my own grandchildren. How I delight in telling them they are smart, funny, kindhearted, and most of all, loved. I enjoy taking them places and buying them things, but perhaps my greatest gift is in knowing they will never be touched by the scars of their grandfather. That curse was forever lifted, the day I forgave my dad. With God's help, I chose to forgive my way to freedom.

With God's help, you can forgive your way to freedom too.

The Power of Forgiveness

When the subject of forgiveness comes up, many people become uncomfortable and even defensive because this may represent unfinished business in their lives. They recognize that forgiveness may require opening old wounds or dealing with people they are trying to avoid or forget. Still others have dismissed the possibility of forgiveness entirely and feel justified to remain in their anger, bitterness, and resentment because of the pain that was once inflicted on them.

I want to encourage you to think about forgiveness in an entirely different way. I want you to consider the power it has to revolutionize your life. You and I have access to enormous power when we forgive. The Bible says that "God is able to do far more than we could ever ask for or imagine. He does everything by his power that is working in us" (Eph. 3:20 NIrv). Reflect for a moment on the magnitude and power of forgiveness. Forgiveness

- lets you experience God's presence like never before
- transforms your entire life
- removes obstacles to joy, peace, and freedom
- improves your spiritual, emotional, and physical health
- restores broken relationships
- reconciles bad marriages
- heals hurting families
- unites divided companies or churches
- rebuilds crumbling nations
- changes the whole world

And the reason it has so much power is because when we forgive, we are most like God!

Unleash the Power
God Has Already Given You

When Jesus was teaching the disciples about forgiveness, they asked that He increase their faith. He told them, "If you have faith as small as a mustard seed, you can say to this mulberry tree, 'Be uprooted and planted in the sea,' and it will obey you" (Luke 17:6). Everyone has the faith of a tiny mustard seed. Jesus is telling us that we don't need more faith to forgive; we need to use the faith we already have. In the same way, we don't need more of God's power to forgive; we need to unleash the power He has already given to us!

Acts 1:8 says, "You will receive *power* when the Holy Spirit comes on you." The apostle Paul wrote in 2 Timothy 1:7, "God has not given us a spirit of fear, but of *power* and of love and of a sound mind" (NKJV). You already have the *power* within you to forgive your way to freedom, and this book will show you how to unleash it.

It is my honor to walk with you step-by-step for a full and complete understanding of forgiveness, to help you resolve your pain of the past once and for all, to have peace now, and to experience the amazing benefits and rewards that are yours as you rediscover your purpose and hope for the future.

Are you ready to forgive your way to freedom?

Forgiveness Prayer

Dear God, thank You for the amazing gift of forgiveness made possible through Your Son, Jesus. Help me have a complete understanding and appreciation of this issue and to make it a part of my life each day. Give me a soft heart and an open mind to learn how to forgive. Help me as I take these next steps to become more like You by practicing what is closest to Your heart.

Reflect and Discuss

1. How has this chapter caused you to think differently about forgiveness?
2. Alexander Pope once said, "To err is human, to forgive, divine." How is forgiveness divine, and how does forgiving make us most like God?

3. What are the things in your life that are defusing your power to forgive your way to freedom?
4. How are you using the power that is already yours?

Your Turn: Apply What You're Learning

Specifically identify the person(s) you may need to forgive or seek forgiveness from. This will allow you to apply everything you'll be learning to your personal situation. Acknowledge this person and situation to God. Pastor and author Rick Warren often says, "Revealing is the beginning of healing." After acknowledging, ask God to help you in this process. Also seek out a trusted friend or family member who you can talk to and who will help you navigate the forgiveness process. Don't take this journey alone.

CHAPTER 2

The Top Ten Myths of Forgiveness

"The truth will set you free,
but first it will make you miserable."

JAMES A. GARFIELD

Among the many challenges my parents had with our large family was feeding this army on my dad's modest salary. My mother could have written a bestselling cookbook, *101 Ways to Prepare Bologna.* She had to be very creative, but she also had to use cheap substitutes to save money. I was content with instant mashed potatoes. Ice milk was much cheaper than ice cream, and I was happy with the cheap substitute. These knockoffs were all I knew as a kid.

But then one day, I ate real mashed potatoes. And then I tried Häagen-Dazs ice cream. I was no longer content to eat the substitutes. Once you've tasted the real thing, there's no going back to the cheap stuff.

The same is true with forgiveness. We try to resolve deep wounds with quick fixes and cheap substitutes rather than face the truth that can set us free. We do this by accepting myths, which are easier to believe and follow but keep us enslaved. I've worked with hundreds of people over the years, and I've noticed myths keep popping up in how they respond to the idea of forgiving, so let's take a look at the top ten, in no particular order.

Myth 1:
Forgiveness Is Not an Issue for Me

I've met many people who dismiss forgiveness as something they don't need or they believe there is nothing new they can learn about such an old concept. At a recent forgiveness session I was leading, a man told me, "I hope your stuff about forgiveness will help some of the people in our church, but this is definitely not something I need." Interestingly, his wife stood behind him and rolled her eyes in disbelief. He had fallen victim to the myth that states we don't have this issue—either we think we've "forgiven" in the past or we simply don't think we need to offer it, when that may not be true. In this case, his wife definitely knew he hadn't forgiven other people. This myth keeps us stuck because we haven't truly dealt with the deeper issues of what has happened to us.

Fortunately, after my session, the man thanked me for sharing. He realized he had more than one person he was struggling to forgive. That's what happens when we face the myth, see it for what it is, and work to resolve it. Just as that man realized the truth, he was able to open himself to his need to forgive, which set him free.

Part of the allure of this myth is that it brings with it a sense of complacency. Complacency keeps us content with the status quo. I like how Dictionary.com defines it: "a feeling of quiet pleasure or security, often while unaware of some potential danger."[1] How does a sports team of superior athletes lose to an underdog? How does a business that soars in the beginning become stagnant and eventually close up shop? How does a marriage that once thrived end in misery and divorce? Most of the time, the issue was not a lack of talent, skill, or resources. It is because we have become complacent. I see this all the time from people who are so convinced and confident they are living in total compliance regarding forgiveness that they never seriously consider if this may be an issue for them. Consequently, they can drift for years in emotional mediocrity and never experience life to its fullest because they consider forgiveness irrelevant to their lives.

We need to combat this myth with truth. And the truth is we may have thought we had forgiven because we once spoke the words, and yet we still find ourselves stuck. But just saying the words and not doing the hard work that comes with that will not set you free. I must confess that after I'd completed writing the first draft of this book, I realized there were two people I needed to seek out to ask for their forgiveness. Even we "experts" can fall for this myth.

So let me lovingly ask you: Have you truly worked through the difficult process of forgiveness? Is there someone you still need to forgive? Perhaps *you've* hurt someone and you need to seek their forgiveness. My friend, nothing can harden our hearts faster than unforgiveness. And what's worse is we can feel justified to harden our hearts because of the way we've been hurt. As I shared earlier, may God give you an open mind and a soft heart as you walk this journey.

Myth 2:
Forgiveness Is Only for the
Benefit of the One Who Hurt Me

I've heard the old story about two former prisoners of war who stood silently at the great Vietnam Memorial in Washington, D.C., when one asked, "Have you ever forgiven our captors who kept us in prison for so many years over there?"

The other veteran replied, "Never! I will never forgive them for what they did to me!"

His friend put his hand on his shoulder and compassionately replied, "It sounds like they still have you in their prison."

If we are the victims of someone else's abuse, rejection, or exploitation, extending forgiveness to our offender goes against every fiber in our being. It makes no sense to give something so precious to the villains in our story when they've already taken so much from us. And the last thing we want at this point is for someone to suggest that the way we're feeling about the scoundrel who hurt us could be wrong.

But forgiveness is *not* about the person who hurt me, it's more about me. No one grows more, learns more, and benefits more than the one doing the forgiving. When I refuse to forgive, not only do I have to deal with the pain that was inflicted upon me originally, but now I place myself in my own jail cell with bars made of anger and resentment, which makes it even worse. However, I can choose to forgive and set myself free from the pain that would linger in my heart.

That's what Steven McDonald discovered about forgiveness.

Don't think of it as doing a special courtesy for the bad guy in your story. This is about and for you.

In 1986, NYPD officer Steven McDonald was shot three times and left for dead. Though he miraculously survived, he was left paralyzed from the neck down. He and his wife, Patti Ann, had been married for less than a year and she was three months pregnant. Steven became completely helpless for even the most routine of tasks.

After their son, Conor, was born, Steven realized that harboring unforgiveness was not only affecting him—and he didn't want to be a father who was bitter and angry, so he began to pray that God would change him from the inside. "I wanted to free myself of all the negative, destructive emotions that [the] act of violence had unleashed in me: anger, bitterness, hatred. . . . I needed to free myself of those emotions so I could love my wife and our child and those around us."[2]

This journey included forgiving Shavod Jones, the young man who had shot him and was now in prison. As he worked to forgive, not only did he find freedom, but incredibly, the two became friends and corresponded. "I forgave Shavod because I believe the only thing worse than receiving a bullet in my spine would have been to nurture revenge in my heart. Such an attitude would have extended my injury to my soul, hurting my wife, son, and others even more. It's bad enough that the physical effects are permanent, but at least I can choose to prevent spiritual injury."[3]

Offering forgiveness is for our benefit. Don't think of it as doing a special courtesy for the bad guy in your story. This is about and for you.

Myth 3:
Time Heals All Wounds

I once worked with a self-sufficient stud of a guy who was as stubborn as they come. He had no problem calling a plumber if a pipe broke or a mechanic if his car broke down, but when it came to his broken heart, he was convinced it would all work out in time. I marveled at how much unnecessary misery he chose to carry in his life simply because he didn't want to deal with the pain of facing the issue and working toward forgiveness.

While time is an important component of any healing process, some wounds are so deep that time alone cannot heal them. It takes time to recover from the trauma of verbal, physical, emotional, spiritual, and sexual abuse. And yet some people buy into this myth that eventually, if they just wait long enough, the ache will go away on its own and they'll be free.

There are no quick fixes or misguided platitudes to hurry the healing process of a genuine victim. But neither should extended inactivity and neglect be confused for healing.

The truth is that time alone does *not* heal all wounds. There comes a time when we need to take action to seek the healing. That may be through family, our friends, our church, or professional help. Even reading and applying the principles of this book are progressive steps toward the healing and freedom you need.

So yes, give it time and don't rush the process, but at some point, we must take responsibility for our pain and resolve it once and for all. The Bible tells us in Ecclesiastes 3:1–8:

> There is a time for everything,
>   and a season for every activity under the heavens:
>
> a time to be born and a time to die,
> a time to plant and a time to uproot,
> a time to kill and a time to heal,
> a time to tear down and a time to build,
> a time to weep and a time to laugh,
> a time to mourn and a time to dance,
> a time to scatter stones and a time to gather them,
> a time to embrace and a time to refrain from embracing,
> a time to search and a time to give up,
> a time to keep and a time to throw away,
> a time to tear and a time to mend,
> a time to be silent and a time to speak,
> a time to love and a time to hate,
> a time for war and a time for peace.

Is it now time for you to forgive or to seek someone else's forgiveness?

Myth 4:
I'll Forgive When They Apologize

Legendary boxers Muhammad Ali and Joe Frazier thrilled sports fans for years with their battles in the ring, but Frazier's greater scars came from the ugly taunts and biting mockery that Ali degraded him with over the years. Ironically Frazier once lent Ali money when he was broke, and he pleaded to have Ali reinstated back into boxing after Ali served time in jail. And many would argue that it was the epic fights with Frazier that made Ali so great. Yet as Ali rose to American sainthood, Frazier lived his final years in obscurity and bitterness. He kept holding out hope for the day that Ali would apologize for the awful names he called him. Although Frazier ultimately forgave Ali, it wasn't until after years of pain he carried inside.

Though our forgiveness issues aren't as public and well reported as Frazier's, we still cling to that same myth that our offender must repent before we are required to forgive. Anytime we set conditions, we surrender control and become dependent on someone else doing something before we can move on. In essence, we hand over the power to that person. This kind of flawed thinking leaves us stuck indefinitely and can impact other areas and other relationships in our lives.

The truth is, there are no conditions to forgiveness. If you want true freedom, then you must forgive regardless of your offender's response. This is the one thing you get to control. You have no control over your offender's behavior, but you do have total control over how you choose to respond. Don't wait for something that may never happen. Begin the forgiveness process toward freedom now by your power of choice.

Myth 5:
Forgiveness Should Be about Justice

Oftentimes we don't want to forgive because we think forgiveness lets people off the hook. But for this myth, I'm not referring to criminal justice. If you or someone you love has been the victim of a violent crime, you have every right to prosecute the alleged offender to the fullest extent of the law. After due process, seeing the guilty brought to justice can help provide peace and closure. In time after your loss, my hope is that forgiveness can provide you freedom.

When God forgave our sins, He still demanded justice, which is why Jesus died on the cross. The Bible says, "Christ didn't have any sin. But God made him become sin for us. So we can be made right with God because of what Christ has done for us" (2 Cor. 5:21 NIrV). Though God wanted to forgive us, someone still had to pay for our sins so justice could be obtained. Christ's death on the cross allowed God to extend forgiveness *and* justice when we believe that Jesus died for our sins.

Where we go wrong is when we create our own sense of justice and set ourselves up as judge, jury, and executioner. But because of our troubled minds and broken hearts, we are the last person who can administer justice toward someone else. I've encountered so many examples of how someone in a family was genuinely hurt, but their sense of justice was to never speak to the other family member again. Still others have broken off a relationship with someone, and they'll tell everyone else about what happened—except the person who actually hurt them. How is that justice? That's why it is always best for us to do the loving and let God do the judging.

And yet it isn't just not forgiving others because of justice; sometimes we can hold unforgiveness over ourselves for what *we've* done in the past. But the same thing is true: we must forgive ourselves and accept the grace God so willingly offers.

I love the movie *The Mission*. Set in 1740s Argentina among the Guarani tribe, the movie tells the story of a Spanish Jesuit priest, Father Gabriel, played by Jeremy Irons, who works to convert the native people to Christianity. Among his converts is mercenary and slave trader Rodrigo Mendoza, played by Robert DeNiro. Before his conversion, Mendoza made a good living kidnapping the Guarani people and selling them as slaves. Struggling to accept that he has now been forgiven and unable to forgive himself, Mendoza demands a penance as justice for all his evil deeds. So Father Gabriel forces him to carry an extremely heavy load around his neck up the mountains to face the Guarani tribe that he so wronged.

Upon his arrival, Mendoza falls to his knees before the chief of the Guarani tribe as the heavy load tied around his neck spills to the ground at his feet. The chief, who is also a convert of Father Gabriel, fiercely looks down in stoned silence at the guilty Mendoza as his tribe looks on. He grabs a knife and holds it to the throat of Mendoza, who fully expects to receive the justice he deserves. Instead, the chief uses the knife to cut the heavy burden tied around Mendoza's neck to set him free. Realizing what just happened, Mendoza begins to weep tears of joy as the chief and his entire tribe shout in celebration. In this story, they all forgave their way to freedom.

The truth is, justice has absolutely nothing to do with forgiveness and everything to do with mercy. This is such a big challenge for all of us when every fiber in our being is crying out for justice when we've been hurt. Forgiving goes against everything we believe about fairness. If you're still demanding justice for how you've been hurt, is it bringing you the peace and freedom you desire?

Forgiving our way to freedom means letting go of those things we cannot control, especially our expectation for justice. God did not give us justice when He forgave our sins, and we need to extend this same grace to those who sin against us. This doesn't mean those who have hurt us by breaking the law should be allowed to escape justice in a court, but when it comes to personally forgiving them, there is a higher court that can handle this better than we ever could. The apostle Paul put it this way: "Leave room for God to show his anger. It is written, 'I am the God who judges people. I will pay them back,' (Deuteronomy 32:35) says the Lord" (Rom. 12:19 NIrv).

Myth 6:
I Must Forget in Order to Forgive

One of the ways I know that someone has truly forgiven is when they can remember their hurtful story, but without the intense pain or need for vengeance. To think we will somehow forget our pain when we forgive is definitely a myth. God says, "I will forgive their wickedness and will remember their sins no more" (Heb. 8:12). God doesn't forget, but He chooses not to remember or hold it over us, and so can we with others.

The truth is, God knows everything, so it is impossible for Him to forget anything. However, when He forgives us He does not bring up our sins ever again. In the same way, once we forgive someone, that doesn't mean we forget. It means we won't bring up the issue again. That's not to say we won't think about it from time to time, but the less we bring it up, the harder it will be to remember.

We cannot forget but we can choose what we remember. It's like the old man who had a black dog and a white dog that constantly fought. Someone asked him which one won the most. The old man answered, "The one I feed the most on that day." So it is with our thoughts. Will we feed our minds each day with the pain of the past only to keep the misery of the experience fresh, or will we choose to feed our minds with truth, beauty, grace, and forgiveness? The Bible encourages us in Philippians 4:8:

"Whatever is true, whatever is noble, whatever is right, whatever is pure, whatever is lovely, whatever is admirable—if anything is excellent or praiseworthy—think about such things." Which choice do you think will lead to freedom?

Myth 7:
Forgiveness Means Condoning What Happened to Me

I counseled with a single mother who had been abandoned by her boyfriend and forced to raise their daughter totally on her own. He provided no child support but continued to be a thorn in her flesh for years. Her anger was so intense that it was becoming all consuming. Just the mention of his name set off an ever-present bitterness that was killing all hope for joy in her life.

After hearing multiple grievances of her story over a long period of time, I gently challenged her to forgive her old boyfriend. This concept was so unthinkable to her for someone she had grown to hate so much.

"After all he's done to me?" she said. "There is no way on earth I could ever forgive him!" She told me that if she did that, it would be as if everything he'd done was okay. She refused to consider otherwise.

Stop trying to resolve deep wounds with quick fixes and cheap substitutes. Embrace the truth that can set you free.

When we forgive someone, we're changing the present and the future, but we're not changing the past. It's a myth to think that forgiveness somehow rewrites history or that by forgiving we're in essence saying that what happened was acceptable and not that big of a deal. Whatever happened to us still happened—and it was still wrong. Nothing changes the truth of that.

When we forgive, we are not trying to make a wrong thing right or diminish the violation against us. Forgiveness cannot change the past, but it can change the way we *feel* about the past. Our brains don't have a magical delete button we can press to erase our bad memories. We cannot deny them, but we don't have to be controlled by them.

The woman I counseled needed to understand that forgiveness wasn't about the jerk who left her. Forgiving him was not about condoning his inexcusable actions, it was about setting *herself* free. By forgiving, she could evict him from the rent-free space in her mind after so many years and get on with her life. That's what you need to do with those who have hurt you. If you feel that forgiving someone is letting that person off the hook, remember they are not off God's hook.

Myth 8:
Forgiveness Means
I Must Restore My Trust in Them

I'm often asked how we should deal with repeat offenders. That would be someone who violates your trust, says they're sorry, and then goes right back again and again doing the same thing. We can extend forgiveness, but trust must be earned. People can be given second chances but only when they've demonstrated they've earned the right to be trusted. I can forgive you for lying to me, but it will be difficult to trust you again until you've proven you are trustworthy.

Do not be conned by the empty words of temporary regret. You must see actions behind those words. This is especially true if you find yourself in an abusive relationship or marriage. I've met women who endure their husbands' abusive behavior by offering "forgiveness," but then they continue to stick around while he continues the abuse. That is a wrong and dangerous view of forgiveness. If you are in this situation, get out now! I'm not advocating divorce, but I am telling you to physically remove yourself and your family from anyone who is threatening your safety. Forgiveness doesn't mean keeping yourself in a place of danger. There are resources at the end of this book that you can seek for help.

In Luke 3, John the Baptist confronts a number of people who want to go through the religious ritual of water baptism without true repentance and change. He tells them, "Prove by the way you live that you have repented of your sins and turned to God" (Luke 3:8 NLT).

It's a myth to think that forgiving someone means you must immediately give them your trust. Hopefully in time they will earn your trust. You should forgive for your own healing, but you are justified to hold out on resuming a relationship with this person if you do not see tangible evidence that they are truly sorry and they want to change their behavior.

Myth 9:
Forgiveness Is the Same as Reconciliation

This is a good transition from my point about trusting. People often get forgiveness and reconciliation confused, but they are two distinct concepts. While we are instructed to forgive everyone, not all relationships can be reconciled or restored to what they once were. We don't have to be friends, socialize, or even like the other person in order to forgive.

Forgiveness is something you and I can do alone, but reconciliation requires the willing participation of someone else. Hopefully the other person would want to restore the broken relationship as much as we do, but we cannot control the response of anyone else.

They may not want a personal relationship with us or we with them, but we must still forgive them. In some cases, reconciling a relationship may be impossible as the person we need to forgive could be far away, in prison, or deceased.

Couples who divorce often struggle with this myth. Ideally we would strive for some sort of civil relationship even if the marriage cannot be restored. I've seen many examples of parents who use their children as pawns, or the divorced couple cannot even be in the same room with each other. Reconciliation may not be desired, but is it unrealistic to think that we can't at least be forgiving, gracious, and respectful to someone we once loved more than any other person?

The truth is, forgiveness doesn't always result in reconciliation, and in some cases, that's perfectly legitimate. If you've done everything within your power to reconcile a relationship, it is no longer between you and that person. It now becomes between them and God. You may feel badly about how things turned out, but you needn't feel guilty if you've done all you can about the situation. You may also be relieved to understand that not all relationships must be restored. We will deal with this important subject in much greater detail in chapter 10, "Restoring Broken Relationships."

Myth 10: Forgiveness Should Be Easy

As one of eleven kids in our home growing up, we had enough to field an entire football team. And just like a football game, we would experience the rough and tumble of life. Daily squabbles were part of our routine. Several times a day, one of the kids would complain to Mom about something that was said, something that was done, or the worst offense of all—"He's looking at me!" My mother would calmly call me out with my little brother Freddie and say, "Gilbert, tell Freddie you're sorry." I would easily parrot those meaningless words to my brother, and for the moment, there was a ceasefire, but it never lasted.

When it comes to serious offenses of a broken heart, it is downright insulting when we dismiss people with simplistic solutions as we did when we were children. Hurtful actions should not be ignored "like water off a duck's back." We cannot simply "put the past behind us." And whoever said, "Sticks and stones may break my bones but words will never hurt me" *lied*! Forgiveness needn't be overcomplicated, but extending something so precious and costly is never easy.

In the movie *A League of Their Own*, which features the rise of women's baseball during World War II, there's a powerful exchange near the end between the coach, played by Tom Hanks, and his biggest star, played by Geena Davis. Because of some personal complications, she wants to quit the team because "it just got too hard." Her coach's response is awesome.

"It's supposed to be hard," Coach Jimmy Dugan tells her. "If it wasn't hard everyone would do it. The hard is what makes it great!"

The truth is, the "hard" is what makes forgiveness so great. If you struggle to forgive because it isn't easy, then you're on the right track. Forgiveness is not for cowards. It is hard and messy and painful. Forgiveness is for the courageous soul who wants to take back their life and rise above the circumstances that were forced upon them at no choice of their own. Alexander Pope got it right when he said that forgiveness is divine! And when you've done the work, the reward is freedom!

◆

Forgiveness Prayer

Dear Lord, please expose any myths that are keeping me from experiencing freedom through forgiveness. I know You resist the proud but give grace to the humble. And so I surrender my pride and humbly seek Your grace, guidance, and strength. Show me whom I need to forgive, and reveal to me if there's someone whose forgiveness I need to seek.

Reflect and Discuss

1. Which of the forgiveness myths did you find the most surprising? Why?
2. Of the myths about forgiveness, which ones do you struggle with most? Why?
3. Do you recognize any of these myths in others? If so, how can you help correct them?
4. After reading this chapter, in what ways will you practice forgiveness differently?

Your Turn: Apply What You're Learning

Carefully examine all the myths listed and honestly determine if you have fallen prey to any of them. Write out what steps you can take to replace them now with truth and follow through with forgiveness. Remember that forgiveness is hard. Just because you still feel pain or have bad feelings toward someone doesn't mean you haven't forgiven. It's a process that takes time.

CHAPTER 3

The Best Way to Forgive

"Forgive us our sins as we also forgive everyone who sins against us"

JESUS CHRIST, in Luke 11:4 NIrV

Louis Zamperini was a long-distance runner in the 1936 Olympics and somewhat of a celebrity. When World War II broke out, he signed up to serve. He was assigned as a bombardier of a B-24 in the Pacific. During a recon mission, his plane crashed in the ocean, leaving him and two others stranded in the open water. For more than forty days they drifted in a raft, praying and hoping that each day salvation would come. Finally rescuers arrived on the scene—except they weren't friendly soldiers; they were the Japanese. Zamperini and the pilot were taken to "safety," which was actually a prisoner of war camp.

One of the most ruthless prison guards, Mutsuhiro Watanabe, took a vendetta against Zamperini and relentlessly abused him. The abuse was so harsh that, after the war, when he was finally released from the POW camp, Zamperini continued to suffer physically and emotionally. His depression was so deep and his nightmares so horrifying that, to deal with them, he began drinking excessively. Everything seemed hopeless.

Then one night in 1949, Zamperini attended a Billy Graham

Crusade in Los Angeles. He accepted Christ that night and experienced a dramatic transformation. He'd found hope again. His life became so much better and stronger that in 1998 he went to Japan to carry the Olympic torch. While he was there, he felt impressed to visit the brutal guard who had caused so much pain. He wanted to offer his forgiveness. Watanabe declined the meeting. So Zamperini sent him a letter instead.

To Mutsuhiro Watanabe,

As a result of my prisoner of war experience under your unwarranted and unreasonable punishment, my post-war life became a nightmare. It was not so much due to the pain and suffering as it was the tension of stress and humiliation that caused me to hate with a vengeance.

Under your discipline, my rights, not only as a prisoner of war but also as a human being, were stripped from me. It was a struggle to maintain enough dignity and hope to live until the war's end.

The post-war nightmares caused my life to crumble, but thanks to a confrontation with God through the evangelist Billy Graham, I committed my life to Christ. Love replaced the hate I had for you. Christ said, "Forgive your enemies and pray for them."

As you probably know, I returned to Japan in 1952 and was graciously allowed to address all the Japanese war criminals at Sugamo Prison . . . I asked then about you, and was told that you probably had committed Hara Kiri, which I was sad to hear. At that moment, like the others, I also forgave you and now would hope that you would also become a Christian.

Louis Zamperini[1]

How is it possible to forgive someone who had behaved so abominably toward another human being? Zamperini was unable to do that on his own. He needed a strength he didn't possess. He needed God's help. This kind of forgiveness is in the rarified air of the divine. God forgives this way, and Zamperini is living proof that we can also forgive the way God forgives. Outside of forgiving us for our sins, I can't think of anything that pleases God more than when we forgive others. So then it stands to reason that if we want to know the best way to forgive, we need to follow the One who does it best.

God's Perspective on Forgiveness

To understand the high value God puts on forgiveness, one of the best places we can look is to the Lord's Prayer in Matthew 6:9–15. In this famous prayer, Jesus had the Almighty's full attention and the power to grant anything He requested, but Jesus asked only for three things: sustenance, holiness, and forgiveness. He prayed:

"Give us today our daily bread"—sustenance.

"Lead us not into temptation, but deliver us from the evil one"—holiness.

"Forgive us our debts, as we also have forgiven our debtors" —forgiveness.

Of all the things Jesus could have asked for, He chose the three things He considered absolute necessities for our lives. Our bodies need food (daily bread) to survive. Jesus considered holiness a necessity as our obedience will keep us walking closely with God. But notice that Jesus also considered forgiveness right alongside food and our relationship with God. In fact, in the very next verse that follows the Lord's Prayer, Jesus said, "If you forgive other people when they sin against you, your heavenly Father will also forgive you. But if you do not forgive others their sins,

If we want to imitate God, we need to embrace forgiveness. And if we want to please God, we need to practice it.

your Father will not forgive your sins" (Matt. 6:14–15). What an amazing statement of God's perspective about forgiveness.

Forgiveness is about redemption, which we see in God's nature throughout the Bible starting all the way back in the book of Genesis when, at the beginning of time, He dispelled the darkness that engulfed the earth as His Spirit moved upon the face of the waters. Think of it: the first recorded words of the Alpha and Omega of the universe brought order and peace from chaos and confusion. As you take your forgiveness journey, this same God can also bring order and peace from the chaos and confusion that may be part of your painful past.

We further see God's redemptive nature when He confronted Adam and Eve after they sinned in the garden of Eden. He had created the entire universe and everything in it. How difficult would it have been to erase Adam and Eve from existence and simply start over? With every available choice at God's disposal and the power to make it happen, God chose forgiveness.

Seeing the incredible value God puts on forgiveness, it would be extremely important that this would also be a priority in our own lives. If we want to know God, we need to understand forgiveness. If we want to imitate God, we need to embrace forgiveness. And if we want to please God, we need to practice it.

The Forgiveness and Love Connection

Throughout Scripture we see that God forgives because He loves. As 1 John 4:8 tells us, "God is love." And in 1 Corinthians 13, which offers the classic definition of love, the apostle Paul concluded by saying that love is the greatest of all. But love isn't just a nice feeling. True love must be expressed. And if it is not expressed, it is meaningless. In fact, Paul wrote in this same chapter that if we could speak like an angel, know all the mysteries of God, have enough faith to move mountains, or give everything we own to the poor, it would all be worthless if we're not expressing love.

So what does expressing love have to do with forgiveness?

Everything. If God just claimed to love us but didn't demonstrate it, what good would it be? God demonstrates His love to us through His magnificent creation, the revelation of His Word in the Bible, His endless compassion, and His ever-sufficient grace for all our needs. However, there is one way God expressed His love to us that far surpasses every other demonstration—and it has forgiveness written all over it.

John describes it this way: "For God so loved the world that he gave his one and only Son, that whoever believes in him shall not perish but have eternal life" (John 3:16). Eternal life was always God's design for His creation, but our sin became an insurmountable obstacle. God gave us His Son because it was the only way to bridge the gap that sin had created. The sinless life and sacrificial death of Jesus in our place was what created the opportunity for forgiveness with God. And that same life and death are what help empower us to forgive others.

Paul echoed this expression of God's love in the book of Romans: "God demonstrates his own love for us in this: While we were still sinners, Christ died for us" (5:8). What makes this grace so amazing is that Christ died for us "while we were still sinners" even before we asked for forgiveness. God didn't give us justice; He gave us mercy. He expressed His great love by looking beyond what we deserved and giving us what we needed. God chose forgiveness.

Inspirational author Roy Lessin provides this classic summary about the need for God's forgiveness in our lives, which inspires and motivates us to forgive other people:

> If our greatest need had been information,
> God would have sent us an educator.

> If our greatest need had been technology,
> God would have sent us a scientist.

> If our greatest need had been money,
> God would have sent us an economist.

> If our greatest need had been pleasure,
> God would have sent us an entertainer.

> But our greatest need was forgiveness,
> so God sent us a Savior.[2]

Yes, God *is* love, and the greatest demonstration of His love comes to us in the expression of forgiveness. This is also the highest expression of our love today. The two are inseparable. Martin Luther King Jr. once said, "We must develop and maintain the capacity to forgive. He who is devoid of the power to forgive is devoid of the power of love."[3]

Forgive Others the Way God Forgives Us

In 1960, Adolph Coors III, of the famed Coors Brewing Company, was kidnapped and murdered. His killer, Joseph Corbin, was apprehended and given a life sentence. Adolph IV was just fifteen when he lost his dad, and he grew up with nothing but hatred and bitterness for Joseph Corbin.

In 1975, Adolph became a Christian, but he continued to struggle with his intense hatred for his father's killer. It impacted his other relationships and continued to pull him down emotionally—until one day a friend lovingly confronted him about what his unforgiveness was doing to his life and encouraged him to forgive Joseph Corbin. Adolph thought he had forgiven, but his friend persisted and asked if he had gone to the prison to tell Corbin he was forgiven. And even more, his friend challenged Adolph to ask Corbin's forgiveness for hating him so long.

At first, Adolph scoffed at the thought. But he wanted to be open to pursuing God's will in his life, so he began to pray about it. After much prayer for God's strength, Adolph found the grace to go to the penitentiary to meet with Joseph Corbin. Sadly, Corbin refused to see him, so Adolph left him with a Bible and these words written inside: *I'm here to see you today, and I'm sorry we could not meet. As a Christian I am summoned by the Lord Jesus Christ my Savior to forgive you. I do forgive you and I ask you to forgive me for the way that I have hated you.*

Because he was able to forgive, Adolph Coors left that prison a free man.[4]

This incredible act of grace is the kind of forgiveness that gets God's attention. It's a remarkable example of how God forgives us and wants us to forgive others. Ephesians 4:32 says, "Be kind and compassionate to one another, forgiving each other, just as in Christ God forgave you." We often interpret this Scripture to mean that we should forgive because God forgave us. However, when this verse says to forgive "just as in Christ God forgave you," could it also mean to forgive the way God does it? While God's forgiveness may seem like an impossible standard, we can strive to imitate the ways He forgives. Let me illustrate four ways God forgives us to help us better understand how we can seek to forgive others.

God Forgives Immediately

"The LORD is compassionate and gracious, slow to anger, abounding in love. He will not always accuse, nor will he harbor his anger forever" (Ps. 103:8–9). Though it takes time to work through the emotional process of forgiveness, committing to forgive someone should be immediate. God doesn't hold grudges, and He forgives immediately. If we want to forgive the way God forgives, we must do the same. If we don't, we will languish indefinitely in our grudges, which only keeps us from freedom.

God Extends Forgiveness Unconditionally

Some may ask, "Don't I have to ask for forgiveness before God forgives?" To receive His forgiveness requires repentance, but He extends forgiveness without condition. Let me highlight an important part of the Bible verse I shared earlier from Romans 5:8, that Jesus died for our sins *"while we were still sinners."* God didn't say, "Repent and then I'll have Jesus die for your sins." Unconditional forgiveness was already in place; we just have to accept it through repentance. If I die in my sins, it means I didn't accept the forgiveness God was offering me. In the same way, we must extend forgiveness unconditionally even if they never say they're sorry.

God Forgives Completely

"You will again have compassion on us; you will tread our sins underfoot and hurl all our iniquities into the depths of the sea" (Mic. 7:19). Have you ever been on a boat in the ocean? It could be on a cruise, deep-sea fishing, or in the military. Imagine tossing a coin overboard and watching it drop down into the ocean. In doing so, you've not only lost it to the depths, you've put it where it can never be recovered. This is the picture the Bible gives of how God forgives our sins. The psalmist David said that "as far as the east is from the west, so far has he removed our transgressions from us" (Ps. 103:12). As we forgive, we do not harbor resentment. We forgive and then let it go completely.

God Forgives Repeatedly

"Then Peter came to Jesus and asked, 'Lord, how many times shall I forgive my brother or sister who sins against me?

Up to seven times?' Jesus answered, 'I tell you, not seven times, but seventy-seven times'" (Matt. 18:21–22). A man once asked, "How many times do I need to forgive others?" The answer came, "As often as God forgives you."

How often has God forgiven us? I'm guessing probably a lot more than seventy-seven times, as He told Peter. God forgives repeatedly, and He expects the same from us. He wants forgiveness to be much more than a onetime event in our lives. God wants forgiveness to be a lifestyle. Sometimes we need to forgive several people only once, while at other times we may need to repeatedly forgive the same person.

I know that forgiving others immediately, unconditionally, completely, and repeatedly sounds impossible. Keep in mind that this takes time, so we all need a lot of grace in the process. Also remember that the same God who forgives us like this can give us the power to forgive others in the same way. For now, let's start slow and begin the process toward forgiving your way to freedom.

Imagine . . . Forgiveness

Every worthy quest begins with a vision of the final result. In Stephen Covey's The 7 Habits of Highly Effective People, habit number two is "Begin with the End in Mind." Covey describes this as "the ability to envision . . . with our minds what we cannot at present see with our eyes."[5]

A mountain climber is motivated to step higher by visualizing himself at the summit. A student is inspired to complete a degree by envisioning herself in a gratifying career. A dieter is encouraged not to cheat when he sees himself looking and feeling better. As William Arthur Ward proclaimed, "If you can imagine it, you can achieve it; if you can dream it, you can become it."[6] Imagining success is always the first step of the journey, and it is no different when it comes to forgiving or being forgiven.

You may have been hurt so deeply that you consider forgiveness impossible. As I shared in my own forgiveness story about my dad, I had given up hope for years that forgiveness and reconciliation would be possible between us. I was ready to let my dad die without even trying because it seemed so hopeless. Whatever happened to you may seem just as hopeless, and you may feel that your injury or trauma is simply unforgivable. Perhaps you hurt someone else and your relationship seems beyond repair, like it cannot be restored. Consequently, you find yourself "stuck" because the pain lingers, but there appears to be no resolution. But what if there *was a way out?*

If you could imagine forgiveness, how would your life be different? How would today be different?

Studies show that people who are willing to consider forgiveness as an option, who according to Dr. Robert Enright, are "able to make a move toward forgiving, if their heart is able to soften some and they feel somewhat less resentment, there's a substantial improvement in their emotional health."[7] In other words, these clinical studies suggest that if people can at least imagine they are able to forgive or have been forgiven, they start feeling better.

Go ahead—try it. What have you got to lose?

So often our hurtful thoughts and memories drag us down into depression and hopelessness. Why not use this same power in reverse for something good, positive, and healthy?

"Make believe" forgiveness has taken place or that troubled relationship has been restored. Use your mind to embrace how you wish you could feel all the time. Indulge in the momentary peace you are conjuring up in your imagination. Enjoy the relief you feel that this load has been lifted and is now gone. What you did or what was done to you never happened.

How would your life be different? How would *today be different?*

And now imagine . . . what if the peace you're experiencing right now could be true all the time? Many of us can only see the "if only" side of life. *If only* I hadn't been hurt. *If only* this person would apologize. *If only* I could reconcile this relationship. *If only* I could find peace and victory in my life. The reason we get stuck is because "if only" requires the cooperation of someone or something else that is beyond our control.

A more productive exercise would be to replace our "if onlys" with "what ifs." *What if* I could resolve the pain of the past? *What if* I could restore my peace in the present? *What if* I could reclaim my purpose for the future? And now receive this truth: "The Spirit God gave us does not make us timid, but gives us power, love and self-discipline" (2 Tim. 1:7). We are not helpless victims. We may have been at one time, but we don't have to be anymore.

We can continue to live by the fickle demands of our emotions, or we can take control of what we think about, which impacts how we feel and how we will live each day. We were not given a choice about what happened to us in the past, but we do have the choice about how we will respond in the present and toward the future. We can forgive others the way God forgives us. And in so doing, experience true freedom!

Forgiveness Prayer

Dear God, thank You for the amazing gift of forgiveness made possible through Your Son, Jesus. Help me have a complete understanding and appreciation of this issue and make it a part of my life each day. Help me as I take these next steps to become more like You by practicing what is closest to Your heart.

Reflect and Discuss

1. How has this chapter caused you to think differently about how important forgiveness is to God?
2. In what ways are love and forgiveness inseparable?
3. What are some ways you have expressed love through forgiveness?
4. If you've struggled to forgive in the past, how can you at least begin to imagine forgiveness to get you started?

Your Turn: Apply What You're Learning

Take a fresh look at Ephesians 4:32 and see if you're forgiving others the way God is forgiving you. Prayerfully consider if your forgiveness is immediate, unconditional, complete, and repetitive. If not, identify those areas where you might be weak and focus on strengthening them so you can forgive as God forgives. There are few goals in life that are more worthy.

Part 2

LOOK BACK
TO MOVE FORWARD—
RESOLVE PAST PAIN

CHAPTER 4

Count the Costs of Unforgiveness

"Forgiving someone may cost you your pride, but not forgiving them will cost you your freedom."

CHARLES F. GLASSMAN

In Matthew 18:21–35, Jesus tells the story about a man who owed the king an enormous amount of money, which he couldn't possibly repay. He begged for mercy, and the king agreed to forgive him the debt. Shortly after being forgiven, this same man confronted a friend who owed him just a few dollars. Though his friend also begged to be forgiven his debt, the man showed no mercy and demanded the payment.

When word got back to the king, he was furious. He had erased this man's huge debt but this same man couldn't forgive just a few bucks from someone else. So the king had the man thrown into prison and punished until he could pay back his debt.

Jesus closes his story with one of the most harsh, solemn statements we find in the entire Bible. Jesus says, "In anger his master handed him over to the jailers to be tortured, until he should pay back all he owed. This is how my heavenly Father will treat each of you unless you forgive your brother or sister from your heart" (verses 34–35).

Wow, that's heavy stuff. Is Jesus saying that not forgiving others disqualifies us from being a Christian, which directly impacts our eternal destiny? Or is He saying that allowing unforgiveness in our lives creates our own, self-made prison? Whichever it is, unforgiveness is serious business to God, so it must be serious business to us as well.

The Oxymoron of the Unforgiving Christian

An oxymoron is the combination of two words that are normally the opposite of each other, such as *jumbo shrimp, passive aggressive*, or where I live in Southern California, *affordable housing*. An *unforgiving Christian* would have to be on this list as an oxymoron.

Let me quickly say that it isn't our forgiveness of others or anything else we do that earns God's forgiveness of our sins. The Bible says, "God's grace has saved you because of your faith in Christ. Your salvation doesn't come from anything you do. It is God's gift. It is not based on anything you have done. No one can brag about earning it" (Eph. 2:8–9 NIrv). In the same way, to believe that unforgiveness is an unpardonable sin suggests that Christ's death on the cross was not sufficient for all our sins.

I think the more appropriate question is how can anyone claim to be a true follower of Jesus Christ, having been forgiven for all their sins, and not be able to forgive others? Jesus further asked, "If you love those who love you, what reward will you get? Are not even the tax collectors doing that? And if you greet only your own people, what are you doing more than others? Do not even pagans do that?" (Matt. 5:46–47).

The apostle John put it this way: "Whoever claims to love God yet hates a brother or sister is a liar. For whoever does not love their brother and sister, whom they have seen, cannot love God, whom they have not seen" (1 John 4:20).

The reason why God takes such a hard line on forgiveness is simple. He is holy, perfect, and sinless, and yet He has forgiven us of our sins. So how can people who are far from perfect and hardly sinless not be able to forgive other people? How can someone who has experienced the amazing grace of God's forgiveness possibly withhold it from anyone else?

From this we can make two simple conclusions: (1) a true child of God and follower of Jesus Christ forgives; (2) forgiveness is an extremely serious issue with God, and we're on shaky ground when we refuse to forgive. Withholding forgiveness takes a terrible toll far beyond our spiritual health. Just as no one benefits more than me when I forgive, no one suffers more than me when I don't. It affects us physically, emotionally, mentally, and relationally as well.

Creating Our Own Torture Chamber

Looking back at Matthew 18:35—"This is how my heavenly Father will treat each of you unless you forgive your brother or sister from your heart"—I believe Jesus was referring to the prison we create for ourselves with bars of bitterness, anger, depression, resentment, and misery. Withholding forgiveness works much like a jail cell in that we surrender our freedom to the dictates of our emotions or other people. Consequently, we are not free to trust, to engage, to love, or to experience life to its fullest. And if we become numb to our unforgiveness, we may not be aware of the price we are paying.

Have you ever taken the time to examine your monthly phone or cable bill? Check it out sometime, and you'll be shocked at what you're paying. Crazy fees with important-sounding names add up in a hurry, and before you know it, you're paying a big price. Unforgiveness works much the same way. Consider these five areas where you pay a huge price, often without realizing it until after wasted years of misery.

Spiritual Toll

The Message Bible gives a great paraphase of an important truth Jesus taught in Matthew 6:14–15: "In prayer there is a connection between what God does and what you do. You can't get forgiveness from God, for instance, without also forgiving others. If you refuse to do your part, you cut yourself off from God's part." Accommodating unforgiveness in our lives has a definite impact on our personal relationship with God.

God's love remains constant and faithful, but our relationship suffers. The Bible says, "Surely the arm of the LORD is not too short to save, nor his ear too dull to hear. But your iniquities have separated you from your God; your sins have hidden his face from you, so that he will not hear" (Isa. 59:1–2). If you feel your worship to God has become shallow and empty or that your prayers seem unheard and unanswered, could it be that there is someone you're struggling to forgive?

As we pull away from God, our hearts become hardened, which is the perfect nesting place for unforgiveness and other sins. In an attempt to fill the gap we created with God or temporarily deaden the pain of our emptiness, we open ourselves up to all kinds of unhealthy and unholy alternatives that drive us even further from God. This can include removing ourselves from church or becoming enslaved to a whole host of addictive behaviors, such as food, alcohol, or sexual sin.

I was once counseling a man who had been struggling to forgive for years over something someone said to him. He confessed, "Every time I think about what was said to me, it eats me up inside!" Frankly, I couldn't have said it better myself. Unforgiveness is a cancer to the soul like nothing else, and the toll it takes on us spiritually can be devastating. I urge you to examine your personal relationship with God, and if you've drifted apart, consider if unforgiveness might be an issue that needs to be resolved.

Physical Toll

According to a study published in the *Journal of Health Psychology*, unforgiveness is a leading cause of stress.[1] When we choose not to forgive and continue to live in our bitterness, our physical health is negatively impacted. We can begin to struggle with headaches, ulcers, hypertension, stomach issues, muscle tension, tiredness, and body aches. It also affects our sleep, so our bodies cannot recover due to the lack of proper rest. Ultimately our immune system wears down and makes us vulnerable to all kinds of sickness.[2]

But it gets worse than headaches, tiredness, and body aches. According to the National Institute of Health: "Emotional stress is a major contributing factor to the six leading causes of death in the United States: cancer, coronary heart disease, accidental injuries, respiratory disorders, cirrhosis of the liver and suicide."[3] And up to 90 percent of all visits to primary care physicians are for stress-related complaints.[4] Those could be serious consequences for withholding forgiveness.

We waste time seeking justice or assigning blame instead of moving on with our lives toward being productive and joyful.

A friend once shared with me about her struggle to forgive a previous employer whom she thought unfairly dismissed her from a previous job. After a while, she began noticing how it impacted her sleep, which made her tired all the time. To cope, she began eating lots of sugary snacks for energy, which packed on the weight. Within a few months, she had gone from a vibrant, energetic dynamo to a tired, overweight, and stressed-out victim of her own unforgiveness. It wasn't until she recognized how her unforgiveness was enslaving her that she found the freedom to get her life back on track.

How is your personal health? If you're not where you'd like it to be, is it possible the reason may be because of unforgiveness? You should consider if a challenging relationship could be driving stress in your life that is impacting your health. Forgiveness could be just what the doctor orders for the health you need and desire.

Emotional Toll

When we don't forgive, we are allowing others to determine how we feel emotionally. We become thin-skinned and easily offended. Healthy, creative, and positive thoughts are drowned out by negativity and malice, which makes us dejected, disheartened, and depressed. Sadly, we become preoccupied with seeking vengeance or feeling sorry for ourselves.

I have often seen this modeled in families, and this cycle of dysfunction extends to future generations. When children grow up in such an unhealthy environment, they learn from their parents that this is somehow the normal way to cope when they think life is not fair or when others have done them wrong. My own father's struggle to cope with his version of fairness in life had a powerful impact on my own struggles. But I've had to learn to accept responsibility for my own joy and peace, which is still a work in progress.

We waste time seeking justice or assigning blame instead of moving on with our lives toward being productive and joyful. We begin to compare our lives with others, and we sabotage our hope for contentment because we can't come to terms with the fact that life is not fair and that imperfect people behave imperfectly. How we feel dictates how we face each day, and unforgiveness contaminates our emotional health like a venom to our bloodstream.

If you are struggling emotionally, I encourage you to do an inventory of your relationships to determine if forgiveness might be an issue. By forgiving or seeking forgiveness, you will see an immediate improvement in your emotional health.

Mental Toll

One alternative to forgiveness is choosing to replay the offense that hurt us over and over in our minds. This was true for me as I struggled to forgive my dad. I held onto those painful memories for years and because I kept them so fresh, I would often get reminders. If I struggled to fix something in the house, I could hear my dad standing over me spewing angry insults that the reason was because I was too stupid. If someone would make fun of me for not understanding something, it drilled into my painful history of being mocked for being dumb. Even today I struggle trying to understand a lot of social media tools. And when people tell me, "It's *sooooo* easy!" it only makes me feel even more stupid if I can't figure it out—so I avoid it.

When we hold onto our past hurts and refuse to forgive, it's much like rewinding the tape and replaying it repeatedly, hoping the more we think about it, the better we might feel. This is part of our defense mechanism to keep our grudges fresh and to rationalize why we are somehow justified not to forgive. We also believe the lie that if we replay our hurt enough times, we will discover something new and we will find the peace that keeps eluding us. But it never quite gives us that peace, does it? It just continues to cement the case we believe we have against our perpetrator as we set ourselves up as both judge and jury.

People who struggle with forgiveness will struggle in other areas because they are following the dictates of their own colored perceptions rather than thinking through healthy alternatives or exposing their thinking to others, such as family, friends, or a counselor, who might be able to help. We tend to close our minds to anything that would go against the narrative that we've been hurt and we are the victim. While that may be true, to hold onto this belief indefinitely keeps us from being free.

Consequently, we fail to learn from our pain. And that keeps us from emerging from our experience as a better person. Instead of growing, unforgiveness renders us mentally stagnant in our anger, bitterness, and misery. As we walk through the forgiveness process, we will discover that our painful experience can actually work for us and not against us.

Bestselling author Josh McDowell knows about the mental toll unforgiveness can take on a person. For years while he was growing up, Josh was sexually abused by a worker on his family's farm. Years later when he became a Christian, he shared his story with a Christian confidant. But Josh was stunned when his friend encouraged him to forgive the man who had abused him.

"I hate the man!" Josh said. "I want him to burn in hell!"

Soon his mind became conflicted. He knew his friend was right—he should forgive the man. After all, God had forgiven him so much. Yet he was unwilling to let go of his pain. Over and over he wrestled with the matter, until finally, he realized he didn't want to live under the strain of how it was affecting him mentally. He didn't want this man to have control over his thoughts. So he made the decision that, as difficult as it would be, he was going to forgive.[5]

Though he could have remained stuck as a victim, Josh chose to forgive, and it totally set his mind free. What was meant for evil provided Josh with an incredible depth of love and compassion, which has guided his ministry. And today Josh McDowell has given his message about the truth of Jesus Christ to more than twenty-five million people in 125 countries and has written the bestselling classics *More than a Carpenter* and *Evidence that Demands a Verdict*. He allowed that painful experience to work for him and not against him.

You can become a better person not just in spite of what happened to you, but in many ways, because of what happened to you. What a joy to know that there's nothing that has happened to you that God cannot beautifully redeem.

Relational Toll

When we don't forgive, we are letting someone else run our lives. It could affect where we go or what we do for fear we might run into this person. When you're not free to move about, it feels much like the jail cell Jesus talked about. We miss happy times, social events, and new experiences because "they" might be there. Instead, we isolate ourselves from our biggest fears, which is far from fulfilling God's plan for our lives.

A friend told me about a former coworker who was laid off from her job but later found herself attending a conference where many of her former coworkers were also attending. My friend offered her a $40 ticket for an awards ceremony, of which she was up for several awards. Though she originally took the ticket, she decided not to attend citing that being in the same room with her former coworkers would be too difficult. The woman lost a great opportunity, not only to grow, but also to network and to accept the recognition for her work.

No one benefits more than me when I forgive. No one suffers more than me when I don't.

We take the toxin of unforgiveness into other relationships as well. The anger and bitterness growing inside us spills over onto other people we love and care about, such as our spouse, friends, and coworkers, who did nothing wrong but who sometimes get the brunt of our anger. We also tend to limit ourselves from new relationships in the future because of how someone else hurt us in the past. It's as though other people in our lives must pay the penalty for what someone else did to us because we are unable to forgive.

How has unforgiveness toward someone impacted your other relationships? I must confess there have been times when I've been upset with someone who did me wrong, but I took it out on my wife, Patricia, with prolonged silence or harsh words spoken out of anger. And here's the really crazy part. I will talk to my wife who loves me and has done nothing wrong in a way that I would never talk to the guilty person who actually hurt me. That's inexcusable!

My friend, unforgiveness costs us more than enough with the real villains in our story without it having to bleed onto the ones who love us and want to be in our lives. As you work through your own forgiveness process, limit the damage so it doesn't cost you other precious relationships that are for you and are there to help you, especially God.

We've Been Holding the
Key to Freedom the Whole Time

In this chapter we've dealt with the heavy costs of unforgiveness, but I want to leave you with great news. While we can be tortured in our homemade jail cell through unforgiveness, we've always had the power to unlock our cell and set ourselves free. At any moment we can open the door and walk out. We have the power to make the hurting stop. That key is forgiveness.

Dr. Frederic Luskin is the director of the Stanford University Forgiveness Projects.[6] His extensive research has shown that forgiveness results in more physical vitality, hope, optimism, and the ability to resolve conflict. He has also found that forgiveness results in a reduction of the physical and emotional impact of stress.[7]

In addition to our spiritual well-being, health professionals agree that there are several medical, emotional, and physical benefits to forgiveness. Specifically, here are eight benefits, or rewards,[8] that come from true forgiveness.

1. *Forgiveness can help lower our blood pressure.* By significantly reducing our anxiety when we resolve the pain of the past, it will help lower our blood pressure and balance our heart rate, which delivers even more health benefits to our body.

2. *Forgiveness can help reduce our stress.* As our blood pressure and heart rate improve, our level of stress will begin to reduce, which will not only improve the quality of our life, but can dramatically help extend it.

3. *Forgiveness can help us be less angry.* Because we're no longer feeling overwhelmed by hostile impulses, we can have more control over our anger. This will help prevent blowups or feeling rage over life's inevitable irritants. By forgiving, we can exercise more grace and patience with others around us, especially with our spouses and families, which will greatly improve their lives too.

4. *Forgiveness can help us break free from dependency.* With our painful past resolved as well as the depression that goes with it, we will not be as dependent on other things that used to provide a temporary distraction or relief. It will help us take control of our lives to pursue the purpose we were born to achieve.

5. *Forgiveness can help us sleep better.* When we are struggling with stress and anxiety, fatigue is common and one of our body's worst enemies. Deep, restorative sleep directly impacts every function of our mind and body. With a lifestyle of forgiveness, we will find ourselves enjoying all the benefits of peace and rest.

6. *Forgiveness can help reduce our physical pain.* With all the benefits to our heart, mind, body, and soul, it can have healing virtues to our physical bodies to help reduce chronic pain or other physical challenges that we may have thought were totally unrelated to unforgiveness.

7. *Forgiveness can improve our relationships.* With all the

benefits we have listed so far, can you imagine how our "new and improved" life would impact the other people we are closest to? This will not only greatly enhance our current relationships but it will also open us up to new and healthy relationships. With our anger, bitterness, grudges, and resentment gone, our disposition would dramatically change. No more walking on egg shells, no more sarcasm, no more unpleasant attitudes, and no more unforgiveness. Okay, we may still struggle in these areas, but it won't be anything like it used to be now that we have walked out of our jail cell and are experiencing the joy and power of freedom!

8. *Forgiveness restores our fellowship with God.* This is the greatest benefit of all. The rusty, old pipe that used to be clogged by our sin and that prevented God's blessings from flowing has been replaced with a clean pathway and direct access to God's presence and perfect plan for our lives.

The Bible tells us to "trust and reverence the Lord, and turn your back on evil; when you do that, then you will be given renewed health and vitality" (Prov. 3:7–8 TLB). And then again, "My son, pay attention to what I say; turn your ear to my words. Do not let them out of your sight, keep them within your heart; for they are life to those who find them and health to one's whole body" (Prov. 4:20–22).

My friend, when you count the costs of unforgiveness as you may be sitting in your own self-made jail cell, I urge you to take the key marked *forgiveness* and set yourself free. Forgiving your way to freedom requires effort, but so does holding onto grudges. One leads to endless misery and bitterness while the other leads to joy, peace, and victory. Choose well.

◆

Forgiveness Prayer

Dear Father, I realize that it grieves You if I don't forgive others. I commit to You this day that I forgive _____ _____. I willingly surrender to You any bitterness or malice in my heart that would prevent You from forgiving me. And now I ask that You walk with me through the process of resolving my pain of the past, restoring my peace in the present, and reclaiming my purpose for the future.

Reflect and Discuss

1. What do you think Jesus meant in Matthew 18:34–35 when He talked about not forgiving others?
2. How important is it that a follower of Christ be a good forgiver?
3. In what ways have you experienced the costs of unforgiveness in your life?
4. When you were able to forgive someone who had hurt you, describe how it made you feel.

Your Turn: Apply What You've Learned

If you're struggling to forgive, consider counting the costs in terms of the spiritual, mental, emotional, relational, and physical toll it's taking on you. Ask a family member or trusted friend to help you and make an actual list. After you compile your list, ask yourself what could be worth so great a price.

CHAPTER 5

Show God Where It Hurts

*"Forgive others, not because they deserve
forgiveness, but because you deserve peace."*

JONATHAN LOCKWOOD HUIE

Jesus once said, "Are not two sparrows sold for a penny? Yet not one of them will fall to the ground outside your Father's care" (Matt. 10:29). While this powerful promise offers us much encouragement, we often miss an important reality that affects us. Though the sparrow is within God's care, you'll notice that He doesn't prevent it from falling to the ground. Like the sparrow, none of us are immune to the heartbreaks and disappointments of life. In fact, Jesus assured us that "in this world you will have trouble" (John 16:33).

God does not always intervene or prevent bad things from happening in our lives. And experiencing that reality can leave us feeling confused, bewildered, and trapped in our pain. Sometimes we may even resent God because we think He could have prevented our tragedy, but He didn't.

In your darkest moments you might wonder, *Where was God, with His love and power, when I needed Him most?*

If you've felt that way, you're not alone. The same David who wrote, "The LORD is my shepherd" in Psalm 23 also asked in Psalm

13, "How long, LORD? Will you forget me forever? How long will you hide your face from me? How long must I wrestle with my thoughts and day after day have sorrow in my heart?" (verses 1–2). There is nothing wrong with questioning God, but are our questions an attempt to find answers or are we just venting?

In David's case, he found his answer as he concluded Psalm 13 with these words: "But I trust in your unfailing love; my heart rejoices in your salvation. I will sing the LORD's praise, for he has been good to me" (verse 6). Venting at God doesn't help us resolve our pain of the past, which can sabotage our peace in the present and derail our purpose for the future. It is during these difficult times that we want to draw closer to God and not alienate ourselves by blaming Him for our troubles. Let me offer three alternatives to blaming God for life's disappointments.

First, we have to take responsibility for our own choices and their natural consequences. For instance, I have a good friend who became a Christian years ago and found forgiveness for his sins after years of living a wild life filled with drug and alcohol abuse. Though God has forgiven his sins, he suffers with ongoing health issues for the ways he abused his body. My friend understands this is not God's fault and it is not a part of God's punishment. It is the natural consequences of his own choices.

Second, we have to accept the disappointments of other people's choices, which may also have consequences that impact us. We are hearing far too much these days about horrible shootings of innocent people at the hands of madmen. This is a tragic example of how a surviving family must endure the consequences of someone else's evil choice. We've all been so inspired to see how many of these families do not blame God for the actions of a gunman but seek God for comfort and strength.

Third, we must accept the fact that we are living in a fallen world. Tragedies will happen that are no one's fault but that we still experience because we are subject to the natural limitations of a sinful world with disease, birth defects, injustice, and immorality. This was never God's plan, and one day His plan will be restored for eternity in heaven, where God promises to "wipe every tear from their eyes. There will be no more death or mourning or crying or pain, for the old order of things has passed away" (Rev. 21:4).

We will talk more about being angry with God at the end of the book, but for now, I urge you not to blame God for your pain but to run to Him as your best source of love and comfort. When I skinned my knee or cut my finger as a child, I would cry to my mother and she would lovingly ask me, "Show me where it hurts." Then she would quickly place a bandage on the wound to help it heal and give it a kiss. Just knowing she cared made me feel better. God loves you like that, but even more. As you start walking through this painful journey, the first thing you should do is show God where it hurts.

The Scars on Our Soul

Forgiving your way to freedom starts by identifying those wounds that have yet to be healed. The goal is not to dredge up the past but to clearly identify the source of your pain so you won't ever have to dredge it up again. You may not be totally free from the pain of the past, but you can learn to manage it so that it no longer controls your thoughts, your emotions, and your quality of life.

And so ... who hurt you? What did they do? When you think of forgiveness, what immediately comes to mind? Are you reminded of an event, or is there someone's face or voice you recall with discomfort? What are your wounds?

Though the pain we endure when we struggle to forgive can come in a wide variety of forms, almost every instance has one common denominator: our pain usually comes at the hands of someone familiar to us. In most cases it was someone who should have loved us but instead greatly disappointed us. The psalmist David knew of this kind of betrayal when he wrote, "It is not an enemy who taunts me—I could bear that. It is not my foes who so arrogantly insult me—I could have hidden from them. Instead, it is you—my equal, my companion and close friend" (Ps. 55:12–13 NLT).

Let's start with parents, where all our stories begin. Each of us has learned a lot of life lessons at the University of Mom and Dad, which is where they learned most of their life lessons as they were passed on from past generations. Parenting is one of life's biggest challenges because we don't have the luxury of practicing on someone else's kids before raising our own. Think about it. We are given an amazing gift of life, and it's up to us as parents to get it right on the first try. Often we nail it, but let's be honest, sometimes we don't.

Venting at God doesn't help us resolve our pain of the past.

As a parent myself, I know I did many things right, but other things I wish I could do over. I said some things incorrectly and some things I wish I had said differently. There are other things I did too much or too little, while other things I did just right. Meanwhile, I was learning all these lessons as I was shaping young and impressionable children who would one day become adults with families of their own.

It isn't as though we don't try to get it right. I believe most parents do the best they can under the circumstances. That doesn't always mean it's the best, but it's the best they can do. For example, a single mom who has been abandoned by a dead-beat husband will do her best to raise her children despite not having the advantages or resources of a married couple. It was difficult for my own dad to express love to his children because he never had it as a child himself. Though he came up short in many areas, I know he was doing the best he knew how under the circumstances.

On the other hand, many parents have unresolved issues they bring into their marriages and visit upon their children. Consequently, their poor responses to pain can extend the cycle of heartache and dysfunction to a new generation, which their children can also pass on.

This can take many forms, and they're all ugly. It could be the demeaning poison of verbal abuse, the devaluation of emotional abuse, the brutalization of physical abuse, or the ultimate betrayal of sexual abuse. The actions of our parents may have left us feeling abandoned, rejected, or shamed in a way that we never fully recover from such a deep level of betrayal. We carry those wounds with us, and they play out in our lives as adults.

For others, our wounds may have come from another member of the family and not a parent. It could be a brother or sister, an aunt or uncle, or a stepparent you inherited as a child. Most wounds come from these kinds of close relationships in the home. Was this true for you? Is there a family member who left you wounded and struggling to forgive?

Were you part of a bad marriage that failed? Some statistics suggest that a divorce occurs in America every thirteen seconds, and up to 80 percent of second marriages also end in divorce.[1] Were you forced to raise your children as a single parent? Were you a child of a broken home? According to the latest census, 1,300 new stepfamilies are forming every day, which opens even more relational challenges.[2] Were you part of a blended family and had issues with your new family or stepparent? Are you still working through the pain of these experiences and unable to forgive?

While the family is the source of most of our wounds, the family of God is also a common place for this type of disillusionment. Many folks have been deeply hurt or felt betrayed at the hands of a pastor, priest, or church leader. You had a right to

expect a high level of integrity, only to be disappointed or betrayed. Your wounds may also have come from a fellow church
member who genuinely hurt you, and you're struggling to forgive
this person.

Other wounds come at the hands of a trusted friend—someone you were once close to, shared life with, and enjoyed being
around. A companion who shared your interests, made you
laugh, seemed to care, and was someone you would proudly consider one of your best friends. Something may have happened to
cause a falling-out between you and your good friend. You are no
longer talking and the relationship appears to be beyond repair,
which leaves you grieving but unable to find resolution.

Someone we don't know at all can leave us wounded. Rob-
bery, identify theft, abuse, physical injury, murder of a loved one,
sexual molestation, or rape can come at the hands of a complete
stranger. Research shows that approximately one in six boys and
one in four girls is sexually abused before the age of eighteen.[3] It
is universally agreed that these alarming statistics are probably
underreported because children are too afraid to come forward.

Do the math, my friend. Look at any size crowd, from a massive audience at a football stadium to your local church, and run
the numbers. What you will find is a staggering number of people
who have been broken inside because of sexual sins committed
against them as children. Were you one of these sad statistics
who experienced this ultimate exploitation? How have you been
working through your pain to find the freedom of forgiveness?

Still more wounds can come at our own hands. Bad choices,
destructive behavior, or irresponsible actions may have brought
consequences that often remind us of our failures, and we cannot
forgive ourselves. Sometimes we may take honest mistakes or innocent accidents so personally that we refuse to extend ourselves
any grace. Have you forgiven yourself for some previous action
or do you believe you are not worthy to be loved and forgiven?

Of course, we may hurt someone else and need to seek another's forgiveness. It may be something we said or did and we've avoided dealing with it or have forgotten about it, but the one we hurt hasn't. Could this be you?

The list goes on endlessly. Our wounds come from family, spouses, children, church members, church leaders, bosses, coworkers, associates, business partners, counselors, ourselves, close friends, or even total strangers.

And then there's God. How could God say He loves me and allow me to experience such pain? Where was He with all His mighty power when I was so deeply wounded and betrayed? I have yet to meet an atheist who didn't experience disappointment with God through some sort of personal tragedy. Are you having trouble reconciling with God?

Whatever your wounds, you need to get them out in the open. Clearly acknowledge and identify them. Confess them to someone else. Apply to your wounds all the lessons we will walk through together so you can resolve your pain of the past. But first it starts with showing your heavenly Father where it hurts.

Resolve That You Will Forgive

Have you ever made a New Year's resolution? Last year mine was to stop making New Year's resolutions! We've all resolved to lose weight, get in shape, improve relationships, and make other healthy choices. We start out strong, but after a short time, nearly all of us fail. The reason is simple. It's because we depend on sheer willpower instead of addressing the issues underlying our bad behaviors. In the same way, we can utter the words *I forgive you*, but true forgiveness requires that we resolve the pain of the past.

This doesn't mean we will come up with all the answers before we forgive. It means we will make a commitment to forgive as we learn the answers along the journey. To understand something is to "solve" it. To be "resolved" is to do something about it. It means coming to a definite decision and taking action. Renowned management consultant Peter Drucker once wrote, "Unless such commitment is made, there are only promises and hopes, but no plan."[4]

If I resolve to do something, it requires extra effort on my part. It means I've worked through the thought process of the benefits and challenges, and I'm now ready to take action. The reason it entails resolve is because it will mean doing something beyond my normal activity or natural desire. If it came naturally to me, I would automatically gravitate toward it, but if it involves something that is difficult, I must be resolved to see it through.

Resolve demands strength and courage. Mahatma Gandhi once said, "The weak can never forgive. Forgiveness is the attribute of the strong."[5] We must exercise discipline to stay focused on any great task, especially our desire to resolve our pain of the past. The apostle Paul used the word *resolve* to describe his passion for Christ when he wrote to the Corinthian church, "I resolved to know nothing while I was with you except Jesus Christ and him crucified" (1 Cor. 2:2). We must show this same resolve to forgive our way to freedom.

While we should extend our commitment to forgive immediately, the actual process of forgiving our way to freedom requires resolve, as will working through the pain of our past. It is not a matter of hopelessly mourning our loss but appropriately grieving before we can move on with our lives. Too often we rush this critical step, and the grieving process ends up taking longer than necessary. Sometimes years. So let's take a long and hard look at our pain and clearly identify its source and all the emotions associated with it so we can resolve it once and for all.

Do Our Wounds Ever Heal?

One of the most beautiful aspects of forgiveness is that it has the power to heal our wounds. But how fast this happens depends largely on us. If we wait until we have everything figured out, that time may never come. If we are waiting for time alone to heal our wounds, we may be waiting a long time (remember that myth we discussed in chapter 2?). But if we can be proactive in our own healing, we can greatly accelerate the process.

As we are able to trust God to heal our wounds, we will discover that He chooses to leave our scars. Award-winning novelist Linda Hogan has a beautiful perspective about scars: "Some people see scars, and it is wounding they remember. To me they are proof of the fact that there is healing."[6]

The greatest example of this truth is Jesus. After His resurrection, the disciple Thomas doubted and said, "Unless I see the nail marks in his hands and put my finger where the nails were, and put my hand into his side, I will not believe." When Jesus appeared before all the disciples eight days later, He turned to Thomas and said, "Put your finger here; see my hands. Reach out your hand and put it into my side. Stop doubting and believe" (John 20:25–27).

The goal is not to dredge up the past but to clearly identify the source of your pain so you won't ever have to dredge it up again.

What did Jesus use to confirm to His doubting disciple Thomas that it was really Him? He could have used thunder and lightning, a dazzling display of His mighty power, or a heavenly host of angels, like the ones who announced His birth to the shepherds. Instead, Jesus showed him His scars. So if Jesus still has His scars, why wouldn't we still have our scars?

If God could raise Jesus from the dead, He certainly could have removed His scars, but He didn't. The reason is because God had a greater purpose. The nail-scarred hands of Jesus serve as an eternal testament of God's love for us by giving His Son to die on the cross for our sins. One day I expect to see those same scars when I meet Jesus in heaven, and I will know that I am there because of them. These are not ugly scars. They are symbols of honor, beauty, and love.

God did not cause our scars, but He can redeem them into something beautiful for us. Our scars are a big part of what makes us who we are. Scars can help us to love deeper, care stronger, understand fuller, appreciate greater, and walk closer to God. They can also drive us to anger, despair, bitterness, and misery. We may not have been given a choice of our wounds, but we do have a choice of how we will respond. As international bestselling author Haruki Murakami of Japan once said, "Pain is inevitable. Suffering is optional."[7]

The apostle Paul also knew about scars. After earnestly seeking God in prayer for relief, he later wrote God's response in 2 Corinthians 12:9–10: "Each time he said, 'My grace is all you need. My power works best in weakness.' So now I am glad to boast about my weaknesses, so that the power of Christ can work through me. That's why I take pleasure in my weaknesses, and in the insults, hardships, persecutions, and troubles that I suffer for Christ. For when I am weak, then I am strong" (NLT).

From Scars to Beauty through Forgiveness

One of the most remarkable stories of forgiveness I've ever read is that of a woman affectionately known as the Turkey Lady. Fifty-year-old Vicky Ruvolo was driving to her home in Long Island and was only a block away one night in November 2004 when a car of teenagers coming from the other direction thought it would be funny to toss out a twenty-pound frozen turkey at Vicky's windshield as they passed.

As the frozen turkey crashed through the windshield, it broke nearly every bone in Vicky's face. The damage to her was so great that, at the hospital, she was placed in an induced coma where she remained for a month. After she miraculously survived the crash, Vicky spent the next several months undergoing surgeries and painful rehabilitation.

Nine months after the horrific prank, the teenager charged with throwing the frozen turkey at Vicky now stood in a courtroom where, if convicted, he would face up to twenty-five years in prison. Young Ryan Cushing was moved with genuine tears of remorse as he stood before Vicky for the first time. The witnesses in the courtroom all awaited his sentence for this evil crime. But the entire room gasped when the judge pronounced a sentence of six months behind bars, five years' probation, some counseling, and public service.

Everyone was beyond outraged by this obvious miscarriage of justice, but not Vicky Ruvolo. That's because the reduced sentence was actually her idea. In front of the witnesses, Vicky gave Ryan Cushing a long embrace and gently said, "I forgive you. I want your life to be the best it can be."[8]

"God gave me a second chance at life, and I passed it on," Vicky tells others today. "If I hadn't let go of that anger, I'd be consumed by this need for revenge. Forgiving him helps me move on." Everyone is amazed at how her face, and her soul, has had so much healing. In fact, she can even laugh about it. "I'm trying to help others, but I know for the rest of my life I'll be known as 'The Turkey Lady.' It could have been worse. He could have thrown a ham. I'd be Miss Piggy!"[9]

Now that's freedom! Today Vicky volunteers with the county probation department, talking to other kids and parents about her experience.[10] She is an inspiring example of how God can heal our wounds but use our scars to accomplish a greater purpose.

God can do the same for you regardless of your circumstances. Don't ignore or dismiss your pain. Acknowledging your woundedness is much like a physician diagnosing an ailment. It may be painful, but the purpose is to find the healing and freedom you need. If God loved you so much to let His Son, Jesus, die for you, He will hold nothing back to help you now. Show Him where it hurts.

Forgiveness Prayer

Father God, I confess to You now all the ways I've been hurt. Here are the people who have hurt me, and here is what happened: _____. I need Your deep healing for the wounds to my soul. I want to be better, not bitter. Therefore, I resolve to forgive and to leave this person in Your hands. Today I claim my freedom from the pain of the past, and I will chart a new course of peace and purpose.

Reflect and Discuss

1. What is the difference between wounds and scars?
2. What are the wounds on *your* soul?
3. Do you agree that pain is inevitable but suffering is optional? Why or why not?
4. How have your wounds made you a better person?

Your Turn: Apply What You're Learning

Clearly and deliberately identify each of your wounds from the past. Get them out in the open and into the light. Recognize the details of how you were hurt and by whom. Then take those names and details directly to God. Your heavenly Father loves you and wants to provide the healing you need. He made your heart. He can mend it.

CHAPTER 6

Do You Want to Get Well?

"Forgiveness is about empowering yourself,
rather than empowering your past."

T. D. JAKES

Throughout Christ's earthly ministry, we see the blind receive their sight, the deaf hear, the lame walk, lepers cured, and even the dead brought back to life. Who would say no to the possibility of receiving such miracles? However, in the fifth chapter of John, we see Jesus at the pool of Bethesda confronting a poor man who was lame and couldn't walk. Before Jesus healed him, He asked an odd question: "Do you *want to get well?*"

Jesus usually didn't ask anything when He healed someone. He was moved by the person's faith and performed a miracle. In Matthew 9, two blind men begged to see again. Jesus asked, "Do you believe that I am able to do this?" (verse 28), and when He saw their faith, He restored their sight. At the pool of Bethesda, however, I believe this is the only time Jesus asked if the person really wanted to be healed. Why would Jesus ask such a question?

The full text of the story reveals that this poor man had been in his condition for thirty-eight years. Some folks in the area said that an angel stirred the water at the pool occasionally and people would run to jump in and experience healing. In fact, the pool of

Bethesda was a popular hangout for a great number of disabled people who were lame, blind, or paralyzed. The man explained to Jesus that he had no one to help him get to the pool.

Realizing that other people in his same predicament managed to find someone to help them, and that this had gone on for thirty-eight years, Jesus likely wondered how serious this man was about healing. Hence the question, "Do you want to get well?" Is it possible this man had grown so familiar with his handicap that being well was a scary proposition? As strange as it may sound, was he more comfortable being a victim than potentially being healthy?

There are several reasons why this lame man at the pool of Bethesda might not have wanted to get well. After thirty-eight years of reliance on others, it would mean his whole life would change. He'd have to become independent, need to find work, support himself, change some habits, and need to take responsibility instead of depending on others to take care of him.

I believe there are parallels with forgiveness from this story. We say we want to forgive or may even claim we have forgiven, and yet the issues requiring forgiveness keep coming up. If we are choosing to hold onto our unforgiveness, Jesus may question if we truly want to experience healing and freedom. It may be possible that we have reasons why we don't want to forgive, even though we know we should and forgiveness promises such a better life for us. But if we're ever to move forward and break free, we need to be able to answer Jesus' question to us: "Do you want to be healed?"

The Seven Subtle
Saboteurs of Forgiveness

Over the many years I've spent talking and counseling with people about forgiveness, I've noticed—just as with the myths we discussed in a previous chapter—there are seven specific reasons people withhold forgiveness. These reasons are not always obvious and they subtly sabotage our attempts at joy, peace, and victory. Sometimes they are so subconscious that we don't even realize what's happening or think of them as deliberate choices. But it's important for us to acknowledge them so we don't allow them to keep us from experiencing true freedom. Let's review them and see if you recognize yourself or someone you love in any of these sinful strategies.

1. We Are Not Being Honest about Our Feelings

Let's get real. One of the main reasons we don't forgive is simply that we don't want to. We might say we do and even tell others that we have forgiven, but deep down inside we know we haven't. I've heard people say some of the most awful things about what someone else did to them. I've watched their eyes glare in anger, their faces turn red, their blood pressure rise, their voices get louder, and the scowl on their faces, and then they end their angry tirade about this person with the empty words, "But I've forgiven." Every fiber in their being betrays their words.

What's wrong with being honest about our feelings and admitting we haven't forgiven someone? It doesn't mean we won't ever forgive them, but for the moment, we're struggling. God already knows we're struggling to forgive, and it's probably obvious to those closest to us, so why not stop living in denial and just admit it? We pretend to have forgiven because we think it makes us look good, but we're deceiving ourselves and needlessly prolonging our healing, mostly because of our pride. The Bible says, "God opposes the proud but shows favor to the humble" (James 4:6).

Be honest about your feelings. Talk to others about your struggle and ask them to help you. Have others pray for you to give you strength and direction. You'll find that as you confess your struggle to others, you will begin to experience freedom and healing. The Bible says, "Confess your sins to each other and pray for each other so that you may be healed" (James 5:16). It is a very healthy thing to shed light on something you're carrying in the dark. You may find as you confess the truth of your feelings, you will feel more willing and able to forgive.

2. We Don't Realize the Price We're Paying

Don't you just hate paying hidden fees? Unforgiveness comes with lots of hidden fees that accumulate over time. Life is hard enough without making it more complicated by our refusal to forgive. If we knew the high price we were paying and could see its devastating effects on our emotional, mental, and spiritual health (take a look back at chapter 4 for a refresher on that), we would learn to forgive much sooner. It's like holding a molten lava rock in our hand to throw at someone else, all the while it is burning a hole in our own hand!

Consider the unusual case of Kevin Tunell. When he was seventeen years old, he got behind the wheel after he'd been drinking, and he accidentally hit and killed eighteen-year-old Susan Herzog. He pleaded guilty to involuntary manslaughter and drunk driving. The judge ordered three years' probation and a year of community service. Kevin also agreed to the demand of Susan Herzog's parents that he pay them a dollar per week for every year their daughter lived—eighteen years. Every Friday Kevin would owe a check for one dollar to Lou and Betty Herzog as penance for killing their daughter.

When Kevin was late or didn't pay, the Herzogs took him back to court. He has often expressed his remorse and asked if he could just pay the balance in one lump sum, but the Herzogs have refused.

The Herzog family insisted this was not about revenge but about making sure Kevin Tunell never forgot what he did, and the dollar check was a weekly reminder. What I don't think the Herzogs saw was the high price they were paying. Just as the weekly payment was a reminder to Kevin Tunell, it also kept the pain and anguish of the accident alive for them. Every week they were given a reminder of their daughter's death. As Lou Herzog said, "Susan's death is there every waking moment."[1] While we can't know their motives or whether they were walking in unforgiveness, I can't help but wonder if this is what their daughter Susan would have wanted or if she would have preferred to see her parents forgive this young man and let everyone get on with their lives.

If you are struggling to forgive someone else, I urge you to consider the cost you're paying. This cost also impacts your spouse, your family, your friends, and others around you. What on earth could be worth so great a cost when freedom beckons?

3. We're Waiting for Someone Else to Do Something

Another reason we don't want to forgive is because we are waiting for someone to apologize or at least act sorry for hurting us. Yes, it would make it a lot easier to get closure if our offender repented, but what if that never happens? Anytime we depend on someone else to do something, we are surrendering control of the situation. We are now subject to other people's choices, which means we think we cannot move forward until someone else does something.

Unforgiveness is our subconscious way of evening the score and manufacturing our own sense of fairness.

The person who hurt you may not be aware of the offense, which is why it's a good idea to seek out this person to talk about it. It's likely that it was a misunderstanding that can be easily and quickly resolved. However, this person may know and simply doesn't care. For whatever reason, this person may have fully intended to hurt you, or your offender may be in prison or dead.

The good news is that we don't have to wait for anyone else to do anything before we can forgive. Whatever happened to us was someone else's choice, but how we respond is our choice. If someone has hurt you, the next step is yours. This is how we empower ourselves to take back control of our own destiny and set ourselves free.

4. We Think Withholding Forgiveness Makes the Other Person Miserable

Unforgiveness is partially about making others pay. It's our subconscious way of evening the score and manufacturing our own sense of fairness. We think it gives us power over our offenders. By stewing in our anger and bitterness, we think we'll teach them a lesson about hurting us. When they see that we've pulled away, stopped talking to them, started avoiding them, treated them poorly, and shut ourselves away, they will be as miserable as we are.

However, this is rarely the case. While we're alone in our depression, they're out having fun and are oblivious to our misery. While we are so focused on them, they are not thinking about us at all. In fairness to our alleged perpetrator, it's highly likely they have no idea of the pain they've caused us, but it's also possible this person doesn't care. Though we remain stuck in our gloom, they've moved on. We need to focus on *our* joy and not their misery.

5. We May Be Comfortable Staying a Victim

There is absolutely no excuse for the hurtful offenses put on innocent people, and I condemn those actions in the strongest terms. I have nothing but compassion and respect for those who are earnestly working through their own forgiveness struggle after a serious transgression has been perpetrated upon them.

In the midst of that struggle, though, some of us are like the lame man at the pool of Bethesda. He had a legitimate handicap, but he lay next to the pool that could heal him for thirty-eight years while others in his same predicament were finding healing. No wonder it made Jesus curious about how serious he was about getting healed. Some of us may prefer the ongoing sympathy to victory. Not as much is expected of us if we are victims. We can always blame our shortcomings on what someone else did to us. We don't have to change, we don't have to grow, and we don't have to take responsibility, because we are victims. If we forgive, we can no longer be victims, and for some, that's uncomfortable.

Let me pause here to repeat something I shared earlier because it is important. If you are a victim of abuse, especially physical or sexual, God does not expect you to stay in such a horrible relationship and keep forgiving over and over each time you are abused, only for it to happen again. If you're married to such a person, I'm not recommending divorce, but you absolutely need to find a way to at least temporarily separate yourself and your family from such an abusive environment. You are a true victim of something you neither signed up for nor deserve. Get out of that environment and seek the help you need. It may be counseling, and it may also mean temporary housing and support. If your friends don't believe you, find new friends. You are God's precious child, and He wants more for you. You can find resources for help in Appendix B at the end of this book that can give you the help you need.

> *When we don't forgive, we falsely think it makes our offenders as miserable as us. Though we often think about them, they have moved on.*

6. We've Become Too Familiar with the Pain

There was a time when my wife, Patricia, and I explored the lifestyle of country living. We bought a house on almost three acres of land surrounded by other larger horse properties in the country. Our ranch house was in the middle of nowhere with nothing but peace and quiet all around us—or so we thought. On our first day in the new house, our neighbors up the dirt road began working in their horse barn and started blaring Country Western music from their radio, which blasted throughout the canyon. Hank Williams's song "Your Cheatin' Heart" immediately led to my broken heart.

At first, I was annoyed—even though it was actually just for short sessions each day as they worked in the barn with their horses. As the days passed, however, I became more furious by these noisy ants at my picnic. But as time wore on, I began to notice it less and less. And then a funny thing happened. I began to like it and actually found it calming. It was amazing to me how something that once was so irritating and intolerable had become such a source of comfort over time.

It's possible that some of us have carried our pain and grief for so long that it has become a part of our identity, and in some way, almost a source of comfort because it's so familiar. It has been a constant companion and has shaped our worldview. Our pain has influenced our thoughts, emotions, and behavior for so long that the thought of living without it is intimidating. To forgive would mean our pain is no longer a part of who we are, and then what do we do?

7. We Are Not Ready to Get Well

For several years it was my great privilege to work at the Union Rescue Mission in downtown Los Angeles. It's one of the largest homeless shelters in America. In addition to emergency services of food and lodging, we offered a long-term rehabilitation program to help people become permanently independent. Despite having these wonderful services available, the streets all around our building were filled with addicts and derelicts who refused to come in and get help. Until they were ready to help themselves, there was nothing we could do to help them. They weren't ready to get well.

Sometimes they would come in and start our rehabilitation program for a few weeks, but they would wind up back on the streets. A common expression among the chaplains there was that "they are still digging their hole." When they hit bottom, they would eventually come for help, and we would see some remarkable transformations, but it was only when they were ready to get well.

We all have areas in our lives we'd like to change. We'd like to take better care of our bodies, read more, spend more time with our family, draw closer to God, or make other improvements. All we lack is motivation and discipline, but for whatever reason, we're just not ready. It usually takes some sort of crisis to serve as a wake-up call before we get started.

You may not be ready to forgive. There may be a good reason if you have experienced significant trauma, which requires considerable healing. Forgiveness takes time. How long is entirely up to you. However, the longer you draw it out, the more Jesus may question if you want to get well. But that means you will also postpone the freedom He wants you to enjoy.

If you've been working through forgiveness for a long time, I encourage you to examine your heart to see if you aren't subtly sabotaging the process. Seriously consider if your unwillingness to extend forgiveness is serving some other desire that would not be edifying to God or to yourself. When you confess and work to finally resolve it, you can forgive your way to freedom.

I read a fascinating story recently about an Iranian woman who harbored anger and unforgiveness and finally chose to get well. Her son and another teenager got involved in a street fight when they were both seventeen. The other teenager killed her son. In Iran, they still have public hangings as part of their capital punishment, and so this teenager was sentenced to die by hanging.

Leading up to the execution, people pleaded with the mother to forgive and accept blood money instead of execution, which was allowed under Iranian law. But each time, she rejected the option and she resented all the pressure she was getting to forgive her son's killer. She even said that her son appeared to her in a dream and asked her to forgive his killer, but she refused.

So the convicted murderer stepped onto the gallows, where the executioner placed the noose around his neck. When asked for final words, he begged for mercy.

The executioner placed a blindfold over his eyes, and within seconds of dropping the floor beneath the young man, the mother yelled for him to halt, which according to the law, was within her right. The killer's pleas had moved her heart. He would still have to face a prison sentence but his life had been spared.

She then turned to the crowd and scolded them, "Do you know what I have gone through all these years and how my life became like poison?" She stepped up to the condemned man and slapped him. Later she said, "I felt at ease."[2]

Though she resisted for years, once she forgave, she immediately started feeling well.

How about you? Has your inability to forgive been like a poison? Has it kept you crippled? God is ready to make you well. Are you ready?

◆

Forgiveness Prayer

Gracious Father, I want to be well. I am ready to be healed. Please reveal to me any areas where I may be sabotaging Your perfect will for my life by not forgiving. Cleanse my heart as I surrender my will to follow You. Please continue to reveal Your wisdom to me as I desire to forgive.

Reflect and Discuss

1. Do you think people choose not to get well? If so, why?
2. Do you see evidence of any of the Seven Subtle Saboteurs in your own life? Which ones?
3. What are some areas of your life where you'd like to improve?
4. What is keeping you from accomplishing these improvements?

Your Turn: Apply What You're Learning

Getting well requires an accurate diagnosis of the problem. Start by being honest about your feelings and ask the hard question: *Do I truly want to forgive?* If not, why not? If so, what are you waiting for?

Part 3

LET GO AND LET GOD—EXPERIENCE FREEDOM NOW

CHAPTER 7

No Longer a Victim

*"You are far too smart to be
the only thing standing in your way."*

JENNIFER J. FREEMAN

Kelly Clarkson has remarkable singing talent, but her song "Because of You" could qualify as the national anthem for codependency. Though I like the melody, the lyrics of this song suggest a total victim who is so paralyzed with fear and pain that she can't stray too far from the sidewalk, she must learn to play on the safe side so she doesn't get hurt, she finds it hard to trust anyone, she can never let anyone else in, and she's ashamed of her life because it's empty. And why? Because of *you*! In the song, it's someone else's fault that her life is such a mess.

It's easy for us to fall into the trap that it's because of someone else that we aren't fulfilled, happy, safe, or confident. And yet the first step to restoring our peace is to take responsibility for our own lives. Yes, we may have been victims at one time, but we don't have to stay victims. God tells us that we have not been given the spirit of fear but of power, love, and a sound mind,[1] which runs contrary to our victim culture. The main difference between victims and victors is attitude.

When Groucho Marx was the host of the long-running game

show *You Bet Your Life*, he had a contestant who claimed to be 102 years old. When Groucho asked him his secret to long life, the man replied, "I think the secret of longevity is to be happy. Every day a man wakes up, he has the choice whether he will be happy or unhappy. I have chosen to be happy."[2] In other words, we have to take hold of who we are and not allow what happens to us to determine our outlook, destiny, or joy. Author Chuck Swindoll sums it up this way: "Life is 10 percent what happens to me and 90 percent of how I react to it."

After a generation of awarding participation trophies to kids for just showing up, we have created a victim culture where taking responsibility has become a foreign concept. The school of hard knocks has been replaced with coddled children who do not know how to react to adversity. If anything, many of us avoid adversity at all costs. So we become the endless victim.

How We Play the Victim

The victim mindset plays well for those who refuse to forgive others, and it comes in a wide variety of forms. These behaviors have been honed through years of practice. And for some of us, we have perfected it so well that it becomes the default position without our even thinking about it.

Here are some examples of ways we play the victim and how they serve as obstacles to forgiveness.

We Play the Blame Game

Have you ever noticed how blaming someone else for our problems never solves the problems? We might make ourselves feel better in the moment, but the challenges still persist. When we blame others, we are more consumed with transferring responsibility than with resolving the problem. What a sinful waste of time and energy.

This sorry practice goes back to the very beginning, when Adam and Eve first sinned in the garden of Eden. What did Adam say to God when God confronted him about eating the forbidden fruit? "The woman you put here with me—she gave me some fruit from the tree, and I ate it" (Gen. 3:12). It appears Adam is not only blaming Eve for his sin but also blaming God. Victims do not take responsibility but always seek to blame others for their issues.

Another classic example was after the Israelites had been freed from Egyptian bondage and fled to the wilderness. It was during

Blaming others also helps rationalize the flawed belief that we are helpless victims to our circumstances.

that time that Moses went up to the mountain alone to meet God and receive the Ten Commandments. Amazingly, when Moses returned, the Israelites were worshiping a golden calf that Aaron (Moses's brother and one of the leaders) had made for them. Listen to Aaron's crazy explanation when Moses confronted him about it: "You yourself know how evil *these* people are. They said to me, 'Make us gods who will lead us. We don't know what happened to this fellow Moses, who brought us here from the land of Egypt.' So I told them, 'Whoever has gold jewelry, take it off.' When they brought it to me, I simply threw it into the fire—*and out came this calf*!" (Ex. 32:22–24 NLT).

Aaron first blamed the people for his sin, and then he dug himself even deeper with the preposterous claim that all he did was throw the gold in the fire and, lo and behold, a golden calf came out. *Don't blame me, I'm not responsible!*

If we take a similar approach to forgiveness, we will never find peace and freedom. Instead, we will perpetuate our pain and justify our failure to find healing by blaming others.

Blaming others also helps rationalize the flawed belief that we are helpless victims to our circumstances. This is where many of us get stuck. When we blame someone else for our problems, we are insisting that person must change before our situation can improve. When I fail to act because I'm expecting someone else to do something, I am surrendering control. Author Robert Anthony says, "If you keep blaming others, you give up your power to change."[3] It's time to give up the blame game and take responsibility for what you have power to change.

We Hold On to Resentment

As we develop a lifestyle of blaming others, it begins to degrade into a spirit of resentment. The word *resentment* is derived from the French root *resentir*, which means "to feel again." This happens when we replay our painful past or a hurtful incident over and over in our minds. It's much like a DVD set on an endless loop where we not only relive the moment but we also relive the emotions associated with it, even though it happened a long time ago. We feel that pain again . . . and again . . . and again . . . and again . . .

We can make it worse because in our pain and anger, we may embellish the facts and exaggerate the circumstances of what we're trying to forgive. If we continue to dwell on our resentment, we can add to the original pain by creating new pain over things that may not be true or real. For example, if we've been hurt by something someone once said to us, we can add words or expressions as we recollect it in our minds that weren't actually said or communicated in such a harsh way and that may not have been accurate. From time to time I may resent something my wife says to me, and when I repeat what she says back to her, I sometimes add a few extra stinging words or say it in a derogatory way. She often has to chuckle because it is so far from what she actually said or meant. When we feel angry or hurt, we can exaggerate things in our mind as we stew in our resentment. Unless we make a course correction, we can develop a lifestyle of resentment that will bleed over into every other relationship.

If this describes you, I need to ask you an extremely important question. Don't rush through this one—really think about it. In the thousands of times you have replayed your painful experience in your mind, has it ever once helped you feel better? Has it ever once offered any new insight you hadn't seen before? Has this practice ever once provided relief or peace? And now let me ask you this question. Didn't it hurt enough the first time? What purpose is served by replaying your painful experience over and over in your mind? You've got a one-way ticket to nowhere and it's time to get off that train. It's time to let go of resentment and be set free.

We Carry Gripes and Grudges

When we persist on blaming others, it develops into resentment, and when we continue to nurture our resentment, it degrades into a full-grown grudge that becomes a part of us and can last for years. I'll never forget counseling with an older gentleman who had been deeply wounded by something his younger brother said to him. The words his brother said had hurt him so deeply that he never fully recovered. He hadn't been able to talk to his brother for a very long time. To hear him tell the story with all the fresh pain, I assumed this was something that had happened recently. I was stunned to learn that the hurtful words came when they were little kids, more than forty years earlier!

Did you know it requires more muscles in your face to frown than to smile? It also requires more effort to hold a grudge than to forgive. Holding a grudge is hard work. Keeping it fresh requires constant effort and only generates pain. Meanwhile, the one suffering the most is not your offender, but you. While you may be alone in your misery, the person you're holding a grudge against is probably out dancing or having a great time.

You may not want to have anything to do with your offender,

but holding a grudge against them is doing the exact opposite of your intentions. When we hold grudges against people, we are not killing them in our minds. We are keeping them very much alive. Unwittingly, we make the person we are trying to avoid into a regular part of our lives. Imagine a picture of you standing next to the person who caused you so much pain and now being handcuffed together. With a grudge, this person goes wherever you go. That's what holding onto grudges and gripes does.

The Lord has a much better way: "Since God chose you to be the holy people he loves, you must clothe yourselves with tenderhearted mercy, kindness, humility, gentleness, and patience. Make allowance for each other's faults, and forgive anyone who offends you. Remember, the Lord forgave you, so you must forgive others. Above all, clothe yourselves with love, which binds us all together in perfect harmony" (Col. 3:12–14 NLT).

Follow the man's example who hadn't forgiven his brother in more than forty years—not in holding a grudge, but in letting it go. After recognizing how futile his grudge was, which he had perfected for decades, I'm pleased to report that he forgave his brother. Today these two are actually close. Wouldn't that be a much better, freer life to have?

We Cry Foul!

One of the main ways we play the victim is by focusing on the fairness issue. We think withholding forgiveness somehow restores a sense of justice and fairness into the equation. We are taught fairness throughout our lives by playing nice, sharing our toys, and minding our manners. We have laws with courts and rules in our games with referees and umpires in an effort to make things fair. When we see an injustice, we have an angry reaction: *That's not fair!*

From every perspective, we have developed a sense of entitlement to fairness. We try to be fair with others and we have the expectation that others should be fair with us. *Life should be fair.* When the natural instinct and trained behavior of fairness is broken, stolen, exploited, violated, or shattered, we feel traumatized. This is why forgiveness feels like the most unnatural reaction to pain or injustice. What happened to us was not fair, and so much of our flesh demands justice.

Withholding forgiveness strokes our human desire to hurt back. You hurt me, so I will hurt you. You hurt me, so I will deprive you of a relationship with me—forever. Because there is no trial, no judge, no jury, no due process, and just our personal judgement, we are able to remain the victim. The best thing to do is release this to God, who is the only one who can judge fairly for everyone involved.

It's important to remember too that we are not an unbiased judge. Surgeons are not allowed to operate on a relative because their personal feelings might affect their ability. A judge would have to recuse himself if a personal circumstance is involved that would prejudice his verdict in a case. Companies cannot do business with other companies if a personal benefit is involved that could be a conflict of interest. It is an honorable thing when we admit we cannot judge fairly because we are too emotionally invested.

This is never truer than when it comes to forgiveness. The person who has been hurt is the last person who can judge fairly. Yes, what happened to us was not fair, but our pain, anger, and fear clouds our thinking and impairs our judgment. We often make things worse when we take matters into our own hands. We need to admit that we are biased and cannot judge fairly. In fact, the Bible offers some great counsel on this very subject:

Never pay back evil with more evil. Do things in such a way that everyone can see you are honorable. Do all that you can to live in peace with everyone.

Dear friends, never take revenge. Leave that to the righteous anger of God. For the Scriptures say, "I will take revenge; I will pay them back," says the LORD. Instead, "If your enemies are hungry, feed them. If they are thirsty, give them something to drink. In doing this, you will heap burning coals of shame on their heads." Don't let evil conquer you, but conquer evil by doing good. (Rom. 12:17–21 NLT)

Victim or Victor: Who Gets to Choose?

Charlie Roberts was a milk truck driver in his community for years and was well known by all the farmers and their families. In 1997, he and his wife lost their first baby, a girl, at childbirth. For years Charlie struggled to forgive God for his loss. For nine years he remained in a victim mindset, until no longer able to cope, on October 2, 2006, he made his way to the West Nickel Mines Amish School in Bart Township, Pennsylvania, to exact his revenge.

Upon entering the school with guns loaded, he ordered all the adults to leave, and later ordered all the boys out of the school. This left him with ten little girls whom he made lie face-down on the floor. He told the girls that he was sorry for what he was about to do. He said, "I'm angry at God and I need to punish some Christian girls to get even with him." He then told the girls, "I'm going to make you pay for my daughter."[4]

Shots fired out as he began shooting the helpless girls, killing five of them. He then turned the gun on himself and committed suicide. The police found his suicide note in which he wrote he could never forgive God. He played a victim to the bitter end of his life.

The very next day, nearly two thousand people gathered for a prayer service. Remarkably, the families who had lost their children because of this man chose a different way. Instead of embracing their victimhood, which would have been un-derstandable, they offered forgiveness to the man who murdered their children. That same day, Amish neighbors visited the Roberts family to comfort *them* in their sorrow

Forgiveness is about using my power. Unforgiveness is about being a victim to someone else's power.

and pain. They invited the Roberts family to the funeral of one of the Amish girls, and at Charlie Roberts's funeral, the largest number of mourners were the Amish.

What was the main thing that separated the man who could not forgive God for his daughter's death and the people who could forgive him for killing their own daughters? Choice. One was a victim; the others were victors. Charlie Roberts's choice led to misery and death. The Amish families' choice led to peace and healing. He made them victims for that one day, but they refused to remain victims. They forgave their way to freedom.

Life will always have its share of challenges and setbacks. People will hurt us and disappoint us. Fairness is elusive and also quite subjective. The difference between someone who suc-cumbs to living as a victim and someone who rises above their circumstances is not a matter of luck or skill. It's the one thing that everybody has and the one thing we totally control. It's en-tirely a matter of choice. How will you choose?

Will you choose to believe that your life is someone else's fault or will you take responsibility for your own life? Will you choose to make excuses for your life or will you look inward with humility? Will you choose to play the blame game or will you seek to find solutions? Will you choose to hold onto your resent-ment or will you stop the cycle of hurting now? Will you choose to continue griping with a negative spirit or will you lay down your grudges? And will you choose to float in whatever direction life takes you or will you take charge of the direction of your life into the future?

Starting today, you can stop being a victim.

◆

Forgiveness Prayer

Heavenly Father, I realize I am not an unbiased judge when it comes to dealing with those who have hurt me. I surrender my desire to hurt back and release my offender to You, dear Lord. Only You are the righteous judge, and I will trust You to work alone, while I seek only to love and forgive those who have hurt me. Thank You that I am no longer a victim.

Reflect and Discuss

1. Can you relate to any of the ways we play the victim discussed in this chapter? Which ones?
2. Do you find yourself reliving the pain of the past in your mind over and over? If so, what have you learned? Have you grown through it? Why or why not? How has it affected you and your relationships?
3. In what ways has your life changed by some of the choices you've made?
4. Would you consider yourself a victim or a victor?

Your Turn: Apply What You're Learning

Admit that you are unable to judge your situation fairly and release your offender to God. Don't waste time waiting for someone else to do something for you to forgive and move on. You may have been a victim at one time, but you are a victim no more. Take your life back!

CHAPTER 8

Don't Lose Your Temper—Find It

"For every minute you remain angry,
you give up sixty seconds of peace of mind."

RALPH WALDO EMERSON

In June 1992, Anthony Colon's unarmed brother was gunned down with thirteen bullets in the East River Projects of Manhattan in New York City. For years he struggled with hate and rage against the three men who murdered his older brother. "It just put so much hate in my life," Anthony said. "I hated everybody. I hated everything. It made me to be . . . like a monster."

As the years passed, Anthony married, started a family, and became a Christian. Along with his faith came a strong desire to find his brother's killer and reach out to him in an amazing spirit of reconciliation. Recognizing how much God had forgiven him, he knew he couldn't hold onto anger toward someone else. So he began to pray that his anger would subside.

Fourteen years later, at a chance meeting while visiting a friend at the Eastern Correctional Facility in Ulster County, New York, he looked across the room and saw Michael Rowe, one of the men who murdered his brother. Instead of feeling hatred, however, he felt peace.

Michael recognized Anthony and immediately looked down.

He had been feeling remorse and shame for years, unable to forgive himself for the murder he had committed, and he feared some sort of violent retaliation.

Instead, Anthony walked over to Michael and said, "Brother, I've been praying for you. I forgave you. I've been praying I would see you again." In that moment of grace, both men found freedom and began a remarkable relationship. Much to the amazement of the prison guards, Anthony even attended Michael's parole hearing to offer his support and helped him secure his release. It's a powerful story that shows how both men found freedom, inside and out, through forgiveness.[1]

Anger is the polar opposite of peace and probably the most powerful emotion related to unforgiveness, which is why I want to spend more time in this chapter than in the others. If we cannot deal with our anger, we will never be able to deal with forgiveness. Instead of losing our temper, we must find it. And then we must deal with it appropriately. As psychologist and world-renowned author Alice Miller said, "Genuine forgiveness does not deny anger but faces it head on."[2]

The Danger of Anger

Ask most people if they have an anger issue and they will say no, but if you ask them if they know an angry person, it's funny how most will say yes. There's a lot of anger out there, but most people have a hard time seeing it in themselves. One reason may be because we presume that anger is an uncontrollable emotion given to violent outbursts.

However, anger has many faces. Depression, cynicism, sarcasm, resentment, jealousy, grudges, bitterness, and negative talk are just a few ways anger can surface in our lives. It's miserable for us and miserable for everyone else around us. Most of all, our anger puts us in an extremely vulnerable position to make terrible and regretful choices. The Bible warns: "An angry person stirs up conflict, and a hot-tempered person commits many sins" (Prov. 29:22).

Here's what we need to understand. Anger itself isn't the problem. It's what we do with the anger that makes it a problem. James isn't stating that we can never be angry—even Jesus was angry (see Matt. 21:12–13 and John 2:13–16). His concern is when we allow anger to consume us.

Anger can serve us well when we apply it properly.

The Bible doesn't condemn anger. In fact, the Bible says, "Go ahead and be angry. You do well to be angry" (Eph. 4:26 MSG). Anger is like fire in that it can work for us or against us depending on the user. Fire can cook our food, warm our home, and provide light in the darkness. And who doesn't love a campfire? However, fire can also consume homes, burn paths of total destruction, and kill anyone in its path when uncontrolled.

Anger can serve us well when we apply it properly. It can be a powerful motivating force for good and push us toward our goals in the face of challenges. It can encourage us to right something that is wrong or fight for justice when something appears unfair. It makes us stronger than normal or more aggressive when we need to be assertive. It can help us move beyond complaining to finding solutions to problems.

When Martin Luther King Jr. saw fellow black citizens being treated as subhuman, he became angry. However, he channeled that anger into the civil rights movement to change the laws regarding equality. When Candace Lightner's thirteen-year-old daughter, Cari, was killed by a drunken driver, she became angry. That anger is what fueled her to change the nation's laws on driving drunk. In fact, she even called her organization MADD.[3]

The problem is not anger. The problem is sustained and unresolved anger that drags on for days, weeks, months, and even years. Let's look again at that passage from Ephesians 4—this time in its full context: "Go ahead and be angry. You do well to be angry—but don't use your anger as fuel for revenge. And don't stay angry. Don't go to bed angry. Don't give the devil that kind of foothold in your life" (verses 26–27 MSG).

Some folks take this Bible passage literally by thinking that not going to bed angry means staying up and fighting! Obviously the deeper meaning is that it's okay to be angry, but the Bible is encouraging us to let it go quickly. Don't hold on to it. Get it resolved. If we don't, we open ourselves up to all kinds of trouble that can greatly complicate a situation that already has enough problems. If you struggle with letting go of anger, think of the hurtful words that have been said, the regrettable actions taken, the devastating choices made, and the relationships ended, all fueled by anger. Uncontrolled anger never brings freedom or peace.

Instead it fans the flames of unforgiveness. Anger can keep the pilot light of our grudges lit for years and prevent us from forgiving others so we'll remain in bondage. Like a fire out of control, it destroys everything in its path. To restore our peace in the present and forgive our way to freedom, we must find and harness our temper.

How Does Anger Get So Out of Control?

A baby is not born angry, so how do we learn anger? It starts with poor modeling from parents who have not learned to control their own anger. If a child is raised in a home where fussing, fuming, or violent outbursts are frequent, this child is taught that anger is not only acceptable behavior, but also the proper way to deal with life's problems.

This was true of me for years. I used to have a violent and explosive temper much like my dad. How I wish I could turn back the hands of time and take back the poundings I gave my poor kid brother, Freddie. I was a bully at school to weaker kids as a way to express my anger. As an adult, I've never been physically abusive to anyone, but I've taken my anger out on my share of inanimate objects that I've punched, kicked, or thrown across the room. As a small child when I saw my dad do these things, I didn't think he was crazy; I thought that was the way people dealt with anger.

My dad rarely used a belt when he punished his children. Taking off a belt took too long. In his anger he mostly used his bare hands. So when I became a father, I reasoned I would never use my hands to discipline my children. The one and only time I used a belt, it left bruises the next day. I was so upset by what I had done that I never did it again. After all these years, it still pains me to think about that. And while some would see me as a monster inflicting child abuse (including me), I thought I was actually doing the right and proper thing as a father because this is what was modeled for me many, *many* times.

If you're someone who struggles with anger, how was this modeled for you by your parents? If poorly, are you passing along this dysfunction to another generation? The good news is that *you* can be the one in your family who makes it stop!

As children, we also learn that anger can be a way of getting what we want. If we cry long enough, we'll get it. Sadly, we often take this pattern into adulthood and believe if we express our anger, we will get our way. We may not throw tantrums but we can complain excessively at work until we get our way. We all know "hot heads" that demand their own way in even the simplest of things, so we give in to avoid an argument. We may make life so unbearable for our spouse that they would rather surrender what they want just to keep peace in the home. This was often my mother's response to my dad's anger. With so many children in the home and no way to support them on her own, she felt trapped to endure his temper until she could finally take no more and they divorced. To this day I don't know how she managed on her own to raise the eight children still living at home. This is why this book is dedicated to her as my hero.

Anger is also an effective way to shield us from the truth. If I'm feeling convicted about something I need to change in my life, anger can help me raise the walls and put up the shield of defensiveness to make it stop. I often see this when I'm talking about forgiveness to individuals or a group. I can mostly see the pain when I counsel with people, but I can often see the anger because they don't want to deal with their pain, so they put up the walls to shut me out. When we do this, we don't learn, we don't grow, and we don't humble ourselves before God who can help heal our pain and anger.

Our anger can serve us well when we apply it appropriately, but leaving it uncontrolled and denying it is like plowing our car through a caution sign at a construction site. Who knows what danger lies just beyond the caution sign that we're ignoring, which can lead to all sorts of regrettable mistakes. It's extremely important that we understand the danger of anger and its devastating consequences.

The good news is that this can also be controlled by your choice. You are not a helpless victim to your temper, but the master of your emotions. Let's see how.

Five Ways to Help You Find Your Temper

Because our reaction to anger is so strong and fast, we often think this emotion is impossible to control, but this is a lie. Can you think of a time when you were angry with someone and in the middle of a heated argument, the phone rang? When you answered it, your tone changed in a heartbeat. You switched from an angry person to a pleasant person in a nanosecond. We've all done that, which proves we can do it if we want to. The question isn't if we should control our tempers, but how. Fortunately, we have practical tools that we can implement and that will transform us from an angry person to a peaceful and joyful person. These are not miracle remedies but learned skills anyone can do.

Delay Your Response

Remember when you were young and got angry? You probably heard an adult tell you to count to ten to calm down. Though counting to ten or taking a "time-out" may seem childish or overly simplistic, the best thing you can do when you are feeling angry is . . . nothing. This means you need to resist the urge to immediately respond if possible. Take a deep breath, and yes, count to ten—or twenty—or one hundred! Wait to respond until you can think and process calmly and clearly. Consider how the Bible phrases it: "The one who has knowledge uses words with restraint, and whoever has understanding is even-tempered. Even fools are thought wise if they keep silent, and discerning if they hold their tongues" (Prov. 17:27–28).

All of our most regretful mistakes are made when we immediately react in anger and do not clearly think through the situation. Giving yourself the space of time will not only keep you from making wrong choices, it will help you make right ones. If we can back away from our anger even for a few minutes, it can make a tremendous difference in how we ultimately resolve our pain. It also allows us to be more open to forgiving.

Your parents may or may not have been good role models when dealing with anger. Fortunately, you have a greater role model in God. Look at these verses of Scripture to discover how God deals with anger:

> The LORD, the LORD, the compassionate and gracious God, *slow to anger*, abounding in love and faithfulness. (Ex. 34:6)

You are a forgiving God, gracious and compassionate,
slow to anger and abounding in love. (Neh. 9:17)

You, Lord, are a compassionate and gracious God,
   slow to anger, abounding in love and faithfulness.
   (Ps. 86:15)

Return to the LORD your God,
   for he is gracious and compassionate,
slow to anger and abounding in love. (Joel 2:13)

I knew that you are a gracious and compassionate God,
slow to anger and abounding in love. (Jonah 4:2)

Do you see a pattern here? James saw it, which is why he declared in James 1:19, "Everyone should be quick to listen, slow to speak and *slow to become angry*." Notice the practical advice James gave in this passage: we should be *quick to listen*, instead of being *quick to react*, which is our natural impulse. Quick to listen requires time to think through our anger and measure it with truth, context, good counsel, and prayer, which will provide a far better resolution than responding in anger.

Think of it as being at a stoplight at an intersection. Red is stop, green is go, and yellow is caution, right? The red light represents what happened in your life that has made you so angry. The green light is what's going to happen next, or how you will react to what happened to you. But the yellow light in the middle between stop and go represents the time you get to choose. The more time you can create and the more truth you can include during the process while you're in the yellow, the better decision you will make when the light turns green.

Determine Why You're Angry

This is how you should spend the time you're creating instead of blowing up in anger. Think of anger as a "signal" that something's wrong, much like a maintenance light on your car's dashboard. It isn't telling you that your car is totaled. It's announcing that something is wrong that needs your attention. Your anger is not telling you that your life is ruined. It's a signal that something's not right and it requires your focus.

When we're angry, it's usually for one of three reasons: we're hurt, we're frustrated, or we're afraid. If someone says something hurtful about me, I can become angry. If I get frustrated after trying to unsuccessfully download some new computer program, I can become angry. If I am afraid I may lose my job, I can become angry.

Here's a great exercise you can do as you are being "slow to anger" and that will help you cool down. When you feel yourself becoming angry, take the time to ask yourself three simple questions:

1. *Am I feeling hurt? If so, what am I hurt about?* Try to determine if the source of your anger is in response to something someone did or said to hurt you. Sort through your thoughts. This may not be what has you angry—in which case, you can rule it out. But if it is, you've now identified the source.

2. *Am I feeling frustrated? If so, what am I frustrated about?* If you're not hurt, you may be angry because you're frustrated about something you feel is beyond your control. Take your time. Think carefully. Can you narrow down the source of your anger to some sort of frustration?

3. *Am I feeling afraid? If so, what am I afraid of?* If you're not hurt or frustrated, something else is lurking out there that has you afraid, which is manifesting itself in anger. Could this be what's driving your temper?

Of course, your source of anger can be more than one of these things simultaneously. You can be hurt and afraid, which makes you frustrated. The point here is for you to determine what is driving your anger and what is the root cause of it. Once you do that, you can then begin to target the source of your anger for resolution, instead of taking it out on someone else.

Focus Your Anger

When we don't target the source of our anger, we often misdirect it toward other people who are innocent but who get the brunt of our criticism, outbursts, or insults. Our anger may be legitimate, but taking it out on other people is inexcusable. We've all done it. We may be angry at someone at work, but we take it out on our spouse. We may be frustrated about a situation and take it out on our kids who have nothing to do with the situation. This is why it is so important that we take time to back away from our anger and determine the true source.

My wife, Patricia, has asked me to try being proactive and tell her in advance if I'm angry or upset about something so she has fair warning and so she also knows that it has nothing to do with her. She tells me that my lips get very thin when I'm angry, so that is her signal. If the Cubs beat the Cardinals in baseball, my lips must get extremely thin!

When I fail and my anger spills onto Patricia, or any other innocent bystander, I try to catch myself before it goes too far. I will apologize to my wife and explain that it's not her, it's a problem at work or a problem person. When I can focus my anger on the proper source, it keeps peace in our home and we can actually work together to attack the problem instead of each other.

Give Your Body a Break

Just as anger affects your mindset, it can also show itself in your body. To help your body get relief from anger, be sensitive to times when you could be vulnerable to anger, such as when you're tired, stressed, hungry, or driving in a car. One of the best things you can do to relieve anger is to exercise. Walking, running, or just moving will invigorate your body and help you feel better and think more clearly. Many times, I have left the house on a walk with something heavy on my mind, and by the time I came home, I had a solution.

Listening to music can help ease your troubled mind. It can be soothing and relaxing music or worship songs that make you feel closer to God. Everyone has

Instead of expressing your anger to resolve your pain, express your pain to resolve your anger.

different taste in music, but filling your head with something soothing and uplifting will help ease your anger. Deep breathing also has a wonderful impact on relaxing you. You can go online and download a wide variety of options for free. You can also find other exercises to help stretch and relax your stressed muscles.

Proverbs 17:22 tells us that "a cheerful heart is good medicine." Laughing is a great antidote for anger. Watch a funny movie or online video, visit a good friend, or try to see the humor in simple things. Though this may not be the solution for your long-term anger, it will get you through today. Sometimes that's enough.

Express Your Anger

Like most profound truths, what I'm about to tell you is both simple and profound, so don't miss it. This simple truth can transform your life.

Instead of expressing your anger to resolve your pain, express your pain to resolve your anger.

Read that again and let it sink in. We know what happens when we have an ugly outburst or spew sarcastic insults because we're angry. This not only doesn't help anyone, it makes an already bad situation even worse. But what would happen if we took time to back away from our anger, identified the source of it, focused our anger on that source, and could explain why we're hurt, afraid, or frustrated to the people who love us?

You've taken a potentially explosive situation or a poison to your soul by internalizing your anger and created the opportunity for true healing, victory, and yes, freedom! And here's the best part of this scenario: Who gets to choose how it will go? You do!

To Feel Different, Think Different

How you feel is in direct response to how you think, especially as it relates to resolving anger so you can forgive. The Bible says in Romans 12:2 that we can be "transformed by the renewing of [our] mind." In other words, we can change the way we think. When we are struggling with anger and can't forgive, it colors our thinking and we remain enslaved to our fickle emotions. Jesus told us that the truth is what sets us free (see John 8:32). So how can we apply truth to the way we think so we can experience freedom from our anger? Allow me to illustrate.

What do you immediately think when someone cuts you off on the freeway? You may think, *This selfish moron is endangering the lives of everyone else on the road. There is no excuse for such recklessness. Where is the highway patrol to give this person a ticket? This person may have a death wish, but I don't want to be killed in the process.*

How does what you're thinking make you feel in that moment? You may feel frustrated or fearful, which leads you to become angry. There you are feeling fine and minding your own business until this jerk cuts you off and now you're upset. Your heart is racing and you wish you could catch up to this guy to give him a good tongue lashing.

Based on what you're thinking and feeling in that moment, what would you do? You might shake your head in disgust, give this person a dirty look, or likely pound on your horn. Here is an incident in which your perspective on the actions of a reckless driver affected what you thought, how you felt, and how you behaved, right?

But what if you discovered that this person was actually rushing to a hospital to save his baby's life who was running a high fever? Ponder on that scene before you answer the following questions.

Would that change your thinking? As a result, would that have changed your feelings and actions? If you knew the full story, you wouldn't be thinking this person was trying to kill you, because you'd understand it was actually a mission of mercy. Your anger would now be replaced by compassion. Instead of honking your horn, you would gladly get out of the way and pray that this driver could get to the hospital in time.

So what changed? How did you go from unkind thoughts, angry emotions, and honking your horn to understanding, compassion, and cooperation? Once you knew the truth, it changed what you were thinking, what you felt, and how you behaved. Knowing the truth did indeed set you free. Now let's apply this same approach to anger and forgiveness.

Advertisers spend billions of dollars trying to get inside your head because they know how you think will dictate how you will behave. That's why they use a sexy woman to sell hamburgers, a movie star to wear their watch, or a famous athlete to sell cereal. Just the sight of golden arches or a swoosh on a shoe affects how we think, which motivates our behavior. None of this is done by accident but through a deliberate branding strategy.

Meanwhile, where do doubt, fear, temptation, and depression come from? They all start with the way we think, but they affect our whole selves. God says, "Temptation comes from our own desires, which entice us and drag us away. These desires give birth to sinful actions. And when sin is allowed to grow, it gives birth to death" (James 1:14–15 NLT).

Once again, we are not helpless victims of our passive thoughts. When dwelling on the pain of our past robs us of our peace in the present, it's time to change the way we think. The Bible promises, "The weapons we fight with are not the weapons of the world. On the contrary, they have divine power to demolish strongholds. We demolish arguments and every pretension that sets itself up against the knowledge of God, and we take captive every thought to make it obedient to Christ" (2 Cor. 10:4–5).

If you struggle with anger or you find this an obstacle to forgiveness from memories of a terrible experience you've been carrying around with you for years, it's due in large part to your stinking-thinking. You can change the way you think and it will change the way you feel—immediately! Life coach Dr. Cherie Carter-Scott put it well when she said, "Anger makes you smaller, while forgiveness forces you to grow beyond what you were."[4]

If you've ever done any serious house painting, you know the bulk of the work is not the splashing of a new color on a house. It is the mundane prep work. Covering the mess with a coat of paint may look good in the short term, but after a while the paint will begin to peel and flake off if you don't do the work of scraping and sanding first. Think of dealing with anger as the prep work for forgiveness.

Don't deny your anger even as you nurture it by holding grudges. Don't continue to waste one more minute with sustained anger at the person you are working to forgive. Eighteenth-century British minister Joseph Hunter reminds us, "My life is in the hands of any fool who makes me lose my temper."[5] Is the fool who hurt you worth surrendering control of your temper? How much more of yourself are you willing to surrender that this person hasn't already taken? If you want to restore your peace in the present, don't lose your temper. Find it!

◆

Forgiveness Prayer

Dear loving God, thank You that You are gracious and compassionate, slow to anger, and abounding in love. I want to be like You, Father. I realize my anger does not bring about the righteous life You desire for me, and so I surrender to You my anger. I do not want to walk in the flesh but walk in Your Spirit as I learn to forgive. As I forgive my way to freedom, help me be free from my anger.

Reflect and Discuss

1. Do you consider yourself an angry person? Would your friends and family agree?
2. Can you think of other dangers that anger causes in our lives?
3. Do you express your anger to resolve your pain, or do you express your pain to resolve your anger?
4. How has anger prevented you from forgiving someone?

Your Turn: Apply What You're Learning

Every time you become angry, ask yourself three questions to get to the source so you can resolve it quickly: What am I hurt about? What am I frustrated about? What am I afraid of? Once you've completed this short exercise, attack the problem and not other people, especially those you claim to love. Remember, they are *for* you, not *against* you!

CHAPTER 9

Remember How to Forget

"When your past calls, don't answer.
It has nothing new to say."

KWINTELL WRIGHT

E lephants never forget." This is one of those old sayings about animals that people don't understand. You've heard people talking about eating like a horse. How many calories can there be in hay? Or sweating like a pig. When was the last time you saw a pig sweat? And my personal favorite is working like a dog. If you saw my little dog Izzy spread out on my favorite chair in the family room you'd wonder where that saying came from.

It might be a stretch to suggest that elephants never forget, but they are known for their impressive memory. These remarkable animals are highly intelligent and extremely social. They not only recognize one another but also recall routes to alternate food and water sources when their usual areas dry up.[1] By the way, contrary to how they're portrayed in cartoons, it's a myth that they're afraid of mice. They just don't like little critters crawling up their trunks. And they hate peanuts.

Sadly, the origin of how an elephant never forgets is how unscrupulous circus trainers used to control these massive animals. They wouldn't use whips or chairs; when the elephants were very young, the trainers would tie a simple rope around one of their legs and then stake it into the ground. This rope was sufficient to keep the young elephant stationary. The elephant would pull and tug but would eventually give up when it appeared futile to keep trying. Many circuses continued this cruel tactic throughout the elephant's life.

A full-grown elephant that had the power to knock over big trees rooted into the ground could be controlled by a simple wooden stake with a rope tied to its leg. It would always think it was impossible to break free based on what the elephant remembered. These circus trainers actually used their memories against them because they knew that *an elephant never forgets.*

For many of us, our painful memories are much like a rope tied to a stake in the ground. Just like this enormous elephant, we could break free at any time, but we are held captive based on what we remember. Since we think we cannot forget our past, it spills over into our peace in the present and sabotages our purpose for the future. Forgetting may be impossible, but what if we could remember in a different way? We cannot change the past, but what if we could recall it in a way that offers peace and hope instead of unresolved pain? We can't forget our hurtful memories, but what if we could manage their frequency and intensity so they do not control us? If we continue dealing with our past in the same way, we will wind up with the same results. It's time for a new way of thinking that will transform our minds.

You Don't Have to Forget to Forgive

As I shared in chapter 2 about the forgive-and-forget myth, let me remind you that God does not forget when He forgives our sins. It is impossible for the all-knowing, omniscient God of the universe to forget anything, and yet it doesn't keep Him from forgiving. God doesn't forget. He *chooses* not to remember. According to research by The National Science Foundation, the average person has up to sixty thousand thoughts each day. Of those, 80 percent are negative and 95 percent are repetitive thoughts.[2] If you've been hurt in the past, how many of your thoughts each day are wasted thinking about something that only brings you pain and is impossible for you to change? How much of your day is spent focusing on the past over which you have no control instead of investing into a healthy future where you have total control? How would your life be different if those percentages were reversed?

One of the most familiar stories of forgiveness is that of Corrie ten Boom. She and her sister were imprisoned in a Nazi concentration camp for hiding Jews. They were treated inhumanely by their Nazi captors, and her sister eventually died in the camp. Corrie had to face the reality of her faith's command to forgive those who had harmed her and her family. She wrote about that experience in her bestselling book *The Hiding Place*.

Years later, although Corrie had forgiven her captors, she still struggled with her memories of that terrible time. A kindly Lutheran pastor comforted and helped her when he told her how the bell in the church tower only rang when someone pulled on the rope. But even after one of the priests let go of the rope, the bell would still ring for a short time and then eventually stop. He explained to Corrie that when we forgive, it's like letting go of that rope. The ringing eventually stops, but if we keep pulling it, it will continue to ring much like pulling the rope on our painful memories.[3] We may never forget them but we can at least make the ringing stop by not pulling on the rope.

We can continue working in vain, trying to forget the grudges, resentment, anger, and misery, or we can work toward remembering in a different way with peace, joy, freedom, and victory. Either option will require time and effort. So which choice do you think makes the most sense? Let's choose to remember in a different way—and gain a fresh perspective.

Dr. Aaron T. Beck is widely regarded as the father of cognitive behavioral therapy.[4] Dr. Beck pioneered many new treatments for clinical depression, including "reframing," which consists of trying to find alternative ways of viewing ideas, events, or situations.[5]

Think of it as seeing events in our lives through a picture frame that we create. If we frame only a portion of the picture, we can leave out important parts that could change the entire perspective. Only by seeing the full picture can we get the whole story. For example, when we begin dating someone, we present a small picture of ourselves. We control what we want the other person to see and do our best to make a favorable impression. That person can't make a very good judgment about us because they have so little information. On a first date we purposely portray our lives in a small frame.

If the first date grows into a courtship, we begin to learn more about each other, both the good and the bad. The frame gets enlarged because we're getting more information. We may like the person we're seeing and want to continue the courtship or we may decide this person is not for us and break it off. If we marry this person, our growing frame now becomes a giant mural where we see everything there is to see about each other.

When teaching on the subject, I like to use a photo I put up on the screen from a vacation trip Patricia and I took to a famous landmark. In the first frame you can only see my face. I ask the group to tell me everything they see in the picture and they quickly conclude that it's only me in the photo. I ask them if there's anything else happening in this photo, but since they can only see me, they might conclude that's all there is to the story. But is it?

I then expand the frame of the same photo, which shows Patricia sitting next to me. Just by enlarging the frame of the picture, they can see there's much more going on. Remember, it's the same photo, but now they are getting more information because they are seeing a broader perspective. I ask if there's anything else going on, but based on what I've shown them, it just looks like Patricia and me sitting together at a table. But is there more to the picture?

That's when I pull back the frame so they can see the whole picture. It's Patricia and me sitting at a table with Niagara Falls thundering in the background. When people see the entire picture, they insist it can't be from the same photograph because it looks so different. It's the exact same picture but just with a much fuller perspective.

Now let's imagine if your hurtful experience could be captured in a large, unframed picture. There would be a lot going on in that picture, but if you're struggling to forget about the past it's because you've framed only a small portion of that picture. Your focus has been on the most painful part and is influenced by your personal bias because of the way you were hurt. That's completely understandable, but it isn't helping you.

If you could enlarge the frame of your picture, would it give you a different perspective? If you and others helping you had more information, could it help you make better choices? And if you could look past your wounds and see everything in the picture, would it help you remember the past differently?

How to Remember in a Different Way

As you reflect on your experience, here are some questions to ask yourself to enlarge your frame and to get a different perspective. You might ask a trusted friend to help you. If you were the victim of a grievous crime, these questions are not meant to minimize your very real trauma, but in most cases, they can help shed light on an incident that has left you hurt and needing to forgive.

Are there any details I may be leaving out of the story because of my hurt and anger?

Can I describe my story objectively?

Is this person aware that they hurt me?

Is there any way I could have misunderstood what was said or done?

Have I made any attempt to reach out to this person to talk about it?

Have I withdrawn from this person?

Do I feel resentment?

Can I express my hurt to resolve my anger?

Do I see my offender as the total villain and myself as the total victim?

Am I in any way responsible for what happened between us?

Are there any other characters involved in this story or just this person?

Can I empathize in any way with the person who hurt me?

Were there any outside influences that made this person do this to me?

What might have happened in this person's past to prompt them to act this way?

What good qualities might this other person have?

Are there good points about this person that other people see?

Am I learning anything new each time I recall the offense?

What effect will my resentment have on my future?

Have I included forgiveness on my list of options?

Do I consider myself more worthy of forgiveness than this person?

This is a tough list that will require some serious and difficult soul-searching. And again, if you have suffered from sexual or physical abuse, please don't think I'm minimizing or in any way alluding to the idea that you may be responsible for what happened to you. I'm not suggesting that at all. However, the more you can enlarge the frame of your story, the more information you can access. And the more truth you see, the sooner you can experience the peace, joy, and freedom of forgiveness. When you include all the details of your story, it will also help you remember the past in a different way.

For example, I counseled with a couple who had been married several years but were now separated. Divorce seemed inevitable. In many of these delicate situations, I've noticed that we often try to make one party the total victim and the other the total villian. Usually the truth is somewhere in the middle. The wife had an affair for which she was genuinely sorry, but the husband was struggling to forgive her. While I wanted to be sympathetic to his pain and not dismiss or rationalize his wife's regrettable decision, I was eventually able to help him explore the bigger picture: he had been a workaholic for years, which contributed to their pulling apart as a couple. While what she did was wrong, he could see how his own behavior contributed to the breakdown. As his view expanded, he was able to forgive her. They reconciled and saved their marriage.

On a lighter note, when I was a pastor, I had a very gracious lady in my church who stopped talking to me. I could tell she was bothered by something, so after a few Sundays of silence,

I approached her after our service and asked her about it. She said I had deeply offended her and her husband. Apparently a few months earlier, while a guest in their home for dinner, they said that I had called her husband a "jiggs."

I drew a blank and asked her to repeat the word. She did and even spelled it for me. I suggested maybe I used the word *jinx* in jest, but they both insisted I used the word *jiggs*. I told them I had no idea what that word meant. Ironically, they didn't either, but they were offended all the same. In retrospect, I should have told them that jiggs meant someone who is brilliant and handsome. Instead, I sincerely apologized for using that word (whatever it meant). When they saw the bigger picture—that I wasn't a villain and hadn't tried to intentionally hurt them—they found it easy to forgive. Though I found that whole episode rather amusing, I admired their willingness to talk with me about it so we could address the problem quickly. If that hadn't happened, the offense would have grown and festered when it was actually very easy to resolve.

Hurt people hurt people.

Empathy:
Taking Yourself Out of the Equation

Sympathy and empathy are kissing cousins, but they are still different. Sympathy is a feeling of care and understanding for the suffering of others. Empathy is the experience of understanding another person's condition from that person's perspective, as though we've stepped into their skin and vantage point. For our purposes, when forgiving, it will help if we can consider empathizing with the person who hurt us so we can understand why this person did what they did to us.

The first step we can take when working toward empathy in forgiveness is to ponder this well-known phrase: *hurt people hurt people.* Read that again and think about it. Usually when someone strikes out to hurt us it's because they themselves are hurting.

My father's abuse of his children was inexcusable, but it helped me forgive and move on with my life as I was able to understand *his* own abusive childhood at the hands of his father. It's possible he thought the kind of excessive punishment he dealt to his children was normal, based on how his father raised him. It actually helped me understand why he behaved the way he did and even helped me have compassion for such a tortured soul. When I was able to empathize with my dad, it helped me forgive him. Again, I wasn't excusing his behavior, but understanding the fuller picture helped me forgive.

Throughout the pages of the Bible we can see that while the writers encouraged empathy (for example, see 1 Cor. 10:24 and Phil. 2:3–4), they did not require it. God understands that, depending on the severity of the offense, empathy in forgiveness is more difficult for some than others. For example, it might be impossible for someone who was raped to have empathy for their perpetrator, which is completely understandable.

Working to gain empathy is not for your perpetrator's benefit. It's for yours. As you are working through the forgiveness process, you might find it helpful to imagine what kind of broken soul would do such an evil thing. How did this person get so messed up that they could hurt you like that?

A young man I worked with really struggled to forgive his mother who was an alcoholic all during his childhood. His father left her when this man was very young, and to cope, his mother turned to liquor. Her drunken binges caused her to lose jobs, which kept them dependent on government assistance. They were in and out of different homes, she had a long string of abusive boyfriends, and she was a constant source of embarrassment to him. All of that fed his rage.

But as he and I worked together in counseling, he was eventually able to look past his own pain and consider what life must have been like for his mother. Imagining life through her eyes helped him forgive her. She was raised by an alcoholic father, abandoned by her husband, and completely stressed out with having this little boy to raise alone. The more he could grasp her misery, the more it helped ease his own misery. As he was able to empathize with his mother's condition and what drove her behavior, it helped him remember the past in a different way.

Our best example of empathy is when Jesus was being led to the cross. He didn't think of how unfair it was that He was being blamed for the sins of the world. He did not seek to retaliate against those who were beating Him, spitting on Him, mocking Him, and cheering His death. Instead, Jesus looked at the crazed mob and simply prayed, "Father, forgive them, for they do not know what they are doing" (Luke 23:34). It was a magnificent prayer of empathy.

A great exercise that can help you build empathy toward your offender is to role-play with a trusted friend. Your friend will play you while you play the role of the person you're trying to forgive. As your friend questions you about what happened, try to give an answer from your offender's perspective. You are not trying to justify anyone's actions, but you will come to appreciate this new perspective as a way to bring you closure. If you seek to understand the brokenness inside your offender that may have motivated certain behavior, it can help you forgive and remember the past differently. This will also help you find the freedom you need.

A powerful illustration of forgiveness through empathy started on the night of July 20, 2012. An excited crowd gathered to watch a midnight showing of the Batman movie *The Dark Knight Rises* in Aurora, Colorado. Just minutes after the movie started, James Holmes, twenty-four, walked into a crowded theater, tossed in a smoke canister, and opened fire with a rifle, a shotgun, and two handguns. When the massacre ended, twelve people were murdered and fifty-eight were left wounded.

One of those fifty-eight was Pierce O'Farrill, who suffered three bullet wounds to his right arm and left foot. He also had shrapnel lodged in his chest. From his hospital bed, Pierce, an active member of The Edge Church in Aurora, near where the shooting took place, was already feeling empathy for the shooter and was ready to extend forgiveness.

"This is going to be hard for people to understand, but I feel sorry for him," Pierce said. "When I think what that soul must be like to have that much hatred and that much anger in his heart—what every day must be like. I can't imagine getting out of bed every morning and having that much anger and hatred for people that he undoubtedly has. I'm not angry at him. I'll pray for him."[6]

It's impossible to forget our past, but we can learn to remember the past in a different way.

When Pierce was released a few days later from the University of Colorado Hospital, he told reporters, "Of course, I forgive him with all my heart. When I saw him in his hearing, I felt nothing but sorrow for him—he's just a lost soul right now. I want to see him sometime. The first thing I want to say to him is 'I forgive you,' and the next is, 'Can I pray for you?'"[7]

Though James Holmes once stood over Pierce O'Farrill's body and shot him three times, intending to murder him in cold blood, Pierce survived and forgave his way to freedom. He later shared in an interview with the *Aurora Sentinel*, "Forgiveness is really more for the victim than the attacker. Forgiveness sets you free. I'm blessed to not know that anger and that hatred in my heart."[8]

Love Our Enemies?

While the Bible may not require us to have empathy for our of-fender, it does challenge us to love our enemy, which also sounds like an impossible task. However, Scripture provides practical in-structions on exactly how we are to accomplish this mission. God says, "Love your enemies, do good to those who hate you, bless those who curse you, pray for those who mistreat you" (Luke 6:27–28). God went even further by having Jesus demonstrate this challenge for us during His life. So we have clear instructions and the perfect model.

What do you think would happen if we did good things for people who don't like us, for people we need to forgive? This might start with our thoughts about them. Consider that God loves them. Remember that Jesus died for their sins too. They are redeemable. If your enemy is a former spouse and you went through a painful divorce, remember that you once found some-thing about this person you loved so much and you married them. Then try moving your thoughts into actions.

Take that difficult coworker to lunch, discover an interest you might share with someone you want to move from an enemy to a friend. Try to be civil and agreeable to an ex-spouse about time with the children. If this is someone who wronged you terribly, perhaps the kindest thing you can do is to stop talking about what an evil person they are, for your own sake. When was the last time you did something kind for someone who may have hurt you?

What would happen if we said nice things to people who only say bad things about us? No matter who it is, everyone loves a compliment. Go out of your way to offer direct and specific com-pliments to people who don't like you. Offer them uplifting words to encourage them. Boast on them in front of other people. One of the reasons they may be so hard to get along with is because they never got the kind of compliments and encouragement you can offer. A word of blessing costs us absolutely nothing but it can be priceless to the one receiving it. Who knows how much their heart could turn if they just knew that someone in the world thought they had value. When was the last time you said something nice to someone who has cursed you?

What would happen if we began praying for the people who have hurt us? We may not be able to change people, but God can. Instead of talking about them behind their back, which accomplishes nothing except to degrade, why not spend that time talking about them to God? He truly cares about you *both* and He has the power to change hearts and circumstances. Can you remember the last time you actually prayed for your enemies by name? Have you *ever* prayed for your enemies?

To start "remembering in a different way," try doing good to those who hate you, blessing those who curse you, praying for those who persecute you, and empathizing with your offender. This will not only help you forgive, but it will help you begin to experience immeasurable healing within yourself, which would overflow onto your enemies to help them find the healing they also need. You'll also find those painful memories becoming less frequent, more distant, and much more manageable. The key is to remove yourself from the center of your universe by reframing the picture, demonstrating empathy, and loving others, especially our enemies. If we cannot forget our painful past, we can at least learn to remember the past differently, which puts us on the road to greater joy, victory, peace, and of course, freedom!

◆

Forgiveness Prayer

Dear God, I do not want to live in the past. I want to receive everything You have for me now and in the future. Give me the courage to reframe my past hurts and wounds to see the big picture. Help me to empathize with my offenders and to love my enemies. Thank You for the clear instructions from Your Word and for modeling this for me through Your Son, Jesus.

Reflect and Discuss

1. What is the connection between forgiveness and forgetting?
2. How did the suggested questions in this chapter help you reframe your picture?
3. In what ways do you think feeling empathy would help you forgive?
4. How are you faring at doing good, blessing, and praying for your enemies?

Your Turn: Applying What You've Learned

Consider if you're being held back by your memories like that poor elephant with his leg tied to a stake in the ground. You have the power to pull up those stakes of your hurtful memories at any time so you can get on with living your life to the fullest, the way God always intended.

Part 4

THE FUTURE IS YOURS—REDISCOVER YOUR PURPOSE AND HOPE

CHAPTER 10

Restoring Broken Relationships

"Never close your lips to those
whom you have opened your heart."

CHARLES DICKENS

O ne of the most majestic places to visit in the United States is Sedona, Arizona. God definitely took His time when He created Sedona. The desert peaks and spires are unrivaled in the old West. My wife, Patricia, and I spent a memorable weekend there with our friends Rich and Lorraine, who own a lovely home in that area. One morning they took us for a hike to enjoy the natural beauty. While the sights were stunning, one location particularly stands out in my mind. We stopped briefly at a local cemetery, and as we wandered around, looking at the tombstones, I noticed this inscription:

> To Our Mother: You spent your life expressing animosity for nearly every person you encountered, including your children. Within hours of his death, you even managed to declare your husband of fifty-seven years unsuited to being either a spouse or a father. Hopefully, you are now insulated from all the dissatisfaction you found in human relationships.[1]

I've never seen anything quite like it. I'm saddened that this mother apparently had issues, but I'm even more disappointed that her children would carve these issues in stone for the world to see forever. What would motivate these children to withhold forgiveness even beyond the grave? While they thought they were getting the last word, it appears their mother still has a hold on their lives.

While most people don't take the trouble to carve their unforgiveness in stone, I've seen many cases where former friends and family members, who were once so close, haven't spoken to each other in years because of a break in their relationship. They have set themselves up as judge and jury and have issued a life sentence of unforgiveness against their offender. In almost every case, the punishment doesn't fit the crime.

God has a better way. We are always required to forgive but also urged to reconcile broken relationships. Just as Christ's death on the cross provides forgiveness for our sins, it also reconciles us back to God so that we may have a relationship with the Father. God wants us to also be reconciled to one another so that our personal relationships can be restored. Let's learn about the role reconciliation plays in the forgiveness process.

What's the Difference between Forgiveness and Reconciliation?

Forgiveness and reconciliation are similar elements but also separate issues. Forgiveness is what I must offer my offender regardless of his or her response. This is something I do alone and for my own benefit. Reconciliation occurs when my offender acknowledges my forgiveness and repents of their actions, with the goal of restoring the relationship to where it was before the offense occurred. I can initiate the forgiveness process myself, but complete reconciliation requires the participation of someone else. As much as possible, reconciliation is the ultimate goal with forgiveness.

What if the person who wronged you needs your forgiveness — and is yearning to reconcile, but doesn't know how?

Just as forgiveness takes time, so does reconciliation. In Luke 15:11–32 Jesus painted a beautiful picture of what reconciliation looks like in the parable of the prodigal son. A wealthy man lost his rebellious son. The son rudely demanded his portion of his inheritance—before his father was even dead—and then left his home and blew through his inheritance in a foreign land.

After losing everything, the son found himself eating in a pig slough to keep from starving. It is there that the Bible says he "came to his senses" and decided to go home and repent to his father. He would say, "Father, I have sinned against heaven and against you. I am no longer worthy to be called your son; make me like one of your hired servants." By the way, this is *true* repentance.

Then comes my favorite part of the story:

> "When he was still a long way off, his father saw him. His heart pounding, he ran out, embraced him, and kissed him. The son started his speech: 'Father, I've sinned against God, I've sinned before you; I don't deserve to be called your son ever again.'
>
> "But the father wasn't listening. He was calling to the servants, 'Quick. Bring a clean set of clothes and dress him. Put the family ring on his finger and sandals on his feet. Then get a grain-fed heifer and roast it. We're going to feast! We're going to have a wonderful time! My son is here—given up for dead and now alive! Given up for lost and now found!' And they began to have a wonderful time." (Luke 15:20–24 MSG)

I believe this father spent every day looking in the distance for his son, hoping he would come home. When he finally saw him, he didn't cross his arms and wait for his son to come crawling to him. Instead, he ran out to meet him, embrace him, and kiss him. When the son started to give the repentance speech he prepared, *the father wasn't even listening.* He had forgiven him already and couldn't wait to reconcile with his son.

In a more contemporary version, I recently read a story from Spain about a father who had a serious falling-out with his son, Paco, and they became estranged for years. In a desperate move to find his long-lost son, he put an advertisement in the local newspaper *El Liberal.* The advertisement read, "Paco, meet me at the Hotel Montana at noon on Tuesday. All is forgiven! Love, Papa." This grieving father hoped and prayed that his son would see it and meet him. When the father arrived, there were more than eight hundred young men waiting at the hotel hoping to reconcile with their father.[2]

Just imagine. What if the person who wronged you needs your forgiveness—and is yearning to reconcile, but doesn't know how? You don't have to wait around hoping. You can be proactive and initiate reconciliation on your own. In fact, this is something God strongly encourages and will empower you to do. He's a God of reconciliation: "All this is from God, who reconciled us to himself through Christ and gave us the ministry of reconciliation: that God was reconciling the world to himself in Christ, not counting people's sins against them. And he has committed to us the message of reconciliation" (2 Cor. 5:18–19).

When Do I Choose Reconciliation?

I've had people tell me they've avoided reconciling with their offender because they mistakenly believed they had to forgive the person and then immediately return to the way things were.

They weren't ready, and that's understandable. We need time to process and grow in our forgiveness.

So when is the right time to choose to reconcile? That's actually simple—when the relationship is more important than the issue that's keeping you apart, try to reconcile. An extramarital affair is a big issue, but a couple can work through it if they believe that saving their marriage is a bigger issue and worth reconciling. Having a friend betray your trust is a big deal, but salvaging that friendship so that trust can be rebuilt may be more important. Forgiveness makes that happen.

Our sin was a *big* issue for God, but His love and desire for a relationship with us was more important to Him than withholding it because of our sin. One of my favorite hymns is "Grace Greater than Our Sin." How I love the chorus:

> Grace, grace, God's grace,
> Grace that will pardon and cleanse within.
> Grace, grace, God's grace,
> Grace that is greater than all our sin![3]

The Bible tells us, "Once you were alienated from God and were enemies in your minds because of your evil behavior. But now he has reconciled you by Christ's physical body through death to present you holy in his sight, without blemish and free from accusation" (Col. 1:21–22). Our sin was an issue. Christ's shed blood on the cross was an issue. However, the larger issue for God was having a relationship with us and so He sacrificed His Son to make it possible. What are we willing to sacrifice to reconcile a broken relationship with someone we care about?

Who Initiates Reconciliation?

Today's culture insists that if you've been hurt, you are owed an apology. The person who wronged you needs to come to you and repent. Perhaps then you might consider forgiving. However, this is contrary to what the Bible teaches. Jesus stated that reconciling with others is something we need to do before we worship God: "If you enter your place of worship and, about to make an offering, you suddenly remember a grudge a friend has against you, abandon your offering, leave immediately, go to this friend and make things right. Then and only then, come back and work things out with God" (Matt. 5:23–24 MSG).

Listen, my friend, God is nobody's fool. We can stand in church, smile as we sing the worship music, make a gift when the offering plate is passed by, and pretend all is great between us and God. But if we are harboring unforgiveness in our hearts toward someone else, our worship is meaningless. It's just for show.

Christ commented further that it is up to us to seek out our offender: "If your brother or sister sins, go and point out their fault, just between the two of you. If they listen to you, you have won them over" (Matt. 18:15). Many offenses can be worked out immediately if we talk to our offender directly. Chances are that person may not know or did not intend to hurt us, and simply talking it through can resolve the problem quickly.

Too often we gossip to other people about the person who hurt us and we wind up talking to everyone around us except the person we should have talked to in the first place. There is never any edifying purpose of gossip. It is always intended to degrade. So unless the person we're talking to is part of the problem or part of the solution, we're just gossiping.

The mistake most of us make is we don't take this step early in the process, and each time we don't reach out to the one who hurt us, it's like laying a brick between the two of you. After a while the bricks begin to pile up. Before we know it, we've created a wall that is now very difficult to break through. That's why we need to reconcile early before we start laying bricks. This is true for any relationship but especially for marriages. Ask any counselor and they will tell you how much easier it would have been if you had come early when there were just a few bricks lying around instead of now having to break down a big brick wall.

With Reconciliation Comes Repentance

While repentance is not required to extend for forgiveness, it is absolutely essential for reconciliation. True repentance requires that someone is genuinely sorry for what occurred, they confess their mistake, and they work to never let it happen again. Unfortunately, there are a lot of cheap substitutes for real repentance, which is downright insulting. Perhaps you've heard it said that if "ifs" and "buts" were candy and nuts, we'd all have a Merry Christmas? Maybe so, but it makes for lousy repentance.

Don't you find it disgusting when someone gives an "if" apology after making some outrageously offensive remark? "*If* my comparison of so and so to Adolf Hitler offended anyone, I apologize." Listen, any time someone begins an apology with the word *if*, you know it's fake.

Adding a "but" in the middle of an apology is also phony. "I'm sorry you were offended, but you took it the wrong way." Here's the rule when someone adds a big but in the middle of a sentence: Everything before the *but* is what was said. Everything after the *but* is what was meant.

Watch for it the next time someone says to you, "I don't mean to complain, *but*..." or, "I don't mean to gossip, *but*..." Somehow we've convinced ourselves that as long as we preface our negative talk by insisting we don't mean to, it somehow makes it okay. True repentance holds nothing back.

Of course, my favorite is what I call the "galactic" apology. Rather than confessing the specific wrong the person has done, they word it more like this: "If at any time and in any way, I might have ever offended you . . . in this life or a previous life . . . on this planet or on some other galaxy, I would like to apologize." That's as endearing as a bouquet of plastic flowers.

For true reconciliation to come about, we need to genuinely forgive and our offender needs to genuinely repent. The level of repentance will determine the level of reconciliation. If it's fake and not heartfelt, reconciliation will likely not happen, or it will be only a surface relationship. If repentance is genuine and humble, the chances are excellent that a broken relationship can be restored. As you work toward reconciliation, here are several traits of true repentance:

Voluntary—not being forced by someone else to do it

Motivated—the goal is reconciliation and not just venting anger

Humility—remembering that we all make mistakes and need forgiveness

Empathy—trying to see and understand the other person's perspective

Responsible—no offering excuses, no explanations, and no blaming others

Specific—not galactic; providing specific details regarding the offense

Transparent—holding nothing back but exposing everything

Vulnerable—working through the risk that an apology might not be received

When I teach seminars on forgiveness, I love to illustrate real repentance using a video clip from the movie *Courage Under Fire*, which tells the true story of Army Lt. Col. Nathaniel Serling.

During the Gulf War, Lt. Col. Serling gives the order to fire on what he thinks is an enemy tank. To his horror, he quickly discovers it is an American tank and that he has accidentally killed his close friend Captain Tom Boylar. The army covers up the details and transfers Serling to a desk job.

The guilt of what he has done and the cover-up haunts him relentlessly. He begins drinking heavily to numb the pain. He separates from his wife and children because he is unable to cope. What turns the whole story around and saves his life is his decision to go to Tom Boylar's parents and repent for what he has done.

In full dress uniform, he goes to their home and in total humility he says, "I want you to know that there was nothing that Tom and I wouldn't do for each other. He was a good soldier. He was like a brother to me." He takes a deep breath and continues, "On that night, February 25, there were enemy tanks in our lines. We thought . . . I thought . . . that Tom's tank was an enemy tank."

As tears roll down his face, he painfully confesses, "I gave the order to fire. God help me, I gave the order to fire. I killed him. . . . As for the funeral, the lies the army told . . . and the lies that I told to you, I can only beg for your forgiveness. As far as that night, I guess there's no way I can begin to ask you to forgive me."

The father looks at Serling with compassion and says, "I know that. But that's a burden you're going to have to put down sometime."

Two remarkable things happen in this scene. First, we see what genuine repentance looks like. Voluntary, humble, motivated, responsible, specific, transparent, and vulnerable. We also see how the forgiveness this gracious and grieving father extends is what sets Colonel Serling free. He quits drinking, he reunites with his wife, and he is able to move on with his life. Such is the power of forgiveness.

How Should Repentance Be Communicated?

Whether you are hoping for repentance from someone who hurt you or if it is you needing to repent to someone else, how this is communicated is vital. It's important to understand the three ways we communicate any message, which are our words, our tone of voice, and our body language. For instance, I can say, "I love you," but if my tone and body language don't match those words, it falls flat. In the movie *Hitch*, Will Smith plays a dating guru and correctly emphasizes that our words represent only 10 percent of our message. Or as he puts it, "Ninety percent of what you're saying ain't coming out of your mouth!"

With this in mind, would email be an appropriate method of reconciling? Absolutely not. That approach should be avoided unless you have no other way. The person on the other end of the broken relationship is just getting your words but cannot see your body language or hear the tone of your voice. Your words are open to the interpretation of someone who is probably already upset with you. Writing a letter is a little more personal because it shows you took the time to write someone on paper and use a stamp, but we're still left with just about 10 percent of the message we want to communicate.

A phone call greatly enhances the opportunity for reconciliation because now the dimension of voice tone is added to the words. The combination of these two elements represents about 50 percent of how we communicate. If it's a simple matter, this will likely work, but if it's a more serious matter and the phone is your only option, make sure the person has time to talk with you. Don't rush through this. So if it's not a good time when you call, tell them you will call them back at a better time. It will be worth the wait.

Of course, meeting with someone face-to-face gives you words, tone of voice, *and* body language, which represents 100 percent of your message. If you want reconciliation to occur, make every effort to meet in person. Once again, make sure they understand you want to have a serious conversation so the time and place is appropriate. You don't want to do this in passing. You want to share when neither of you is rushed.

If someone doesn't want to meet with you, will not take your phone call, or refuses to respond, then be at peace that you've done your part in the reconciliation process. The issue is no longer between you and that person. It's now between that person and God. If reconciling is important to you, then continue to wait as God works on that person's heart. Sometimes people just aren't ready and need more time.

And if someone should ever apologize to you or repent for something more serious—be a good forgiver. If someone tells you they are sorry in an email or a letter, it is inexcusable for you not to acknowledge their effort. Ignoring their message and leaving them in confused silence is not just rude, it's cruel. If you're not ready to reconcile, at least show them enough respect to acknowledge them, perhaps even thank them. Withholding forgiveness is bad enough but to still do it after someone has repented to you is far worse.

When Reconciliation Isn't Possible

While reconciliation is a worthy goal, not all relationships can be restored. It is possible to genuinely forgive someone and not desire or be able to have an ongoing relationship with that person.

For example, if a marriage is shattered by infidelity, the innocent party can forgive but they may choose to end their marriage by divorce. But it doesn't mean divorce is inevitable. Many marriages have survived this tragedy through forgiveness and the desire to reconcile. This is the ideal scenario, yet God understands when you've done all you can and yet reconciliation still

You know it's time to reconcile when you realize the relationship is more important than the issue that broke you apart.

cannot happen (see Matt. 19:9).

If someone is brutally attacked and the culprit is imprisoned for the crime, ideally the victim will learn to forgive for their own personal healing. But because the offender is in jail, it is unlikely that reconciliation can occur or should occur. Some victims have chosen to make this remarkable gesture of grace, but there is nothing wrong with avoiding that person and moving on with your life.

In some cases, the offender might no longer be living, making reconciliation impossible. In this case, I would encourage you to consider writing all your thoughts on paper, and if you go visit that person at the cemetery, read your letter out loud at their tombstone. Though you are not able to reconcile this relationship, there is much healing in resolving whatever was between the two of you in your heart and mind. And then for final closure, burn your letter.

Even if your offender is alive and well, God doesn't necessarily expect you to have an ongoing relationship, especially if this person is a constant source of pain for you. Use your best judgment or seek the counsel of a friend or family member as you navigate this issue. The Bible says, "*If it is possible*, as far as it depends on you, live at peace with everyone" (Rom. 12:18). Forgive always; reconcile if it is possible.

When Reconciliation Changed the World

Racial segregation in South Africa began in colonial times under Dutch and British rule. However, apartheid as an official policy was introduced following the general election of 1948. New legislation classified inhabitants into racial groups, and residential areas were segregated, sometimes by means of forced removals. Nonwhite political representation was completely abolished and black people were deprived of their citizenship. The government segregated education, medical care, beaches, and other public services and provided black people with services inferior to those of white people.

One anti-apartheid revolutionary who stood against this blatant racism was a young politician named Nelson Mandela. His goal was to end the apartheid rule of South Africa and to see his homeland as one democracy where blacks and whites were treated the same. He became the leader of the African National Congress and a threat to the white leadership of South Africa. In 1963, he was sent to prison on charges of trying to sabotage the nation's government.

He spent the next twenty-seven years in prison, most of it on Robben Island off the coast of Capetown, where he endured torture and hard labor. His damp concrete cell measured eight feet by seven feet, with a straw mat on which to sleep.

White prison wardens verbally and physically harassed Mandela and his fellow political prisoners while they had to break rocks into gravel. In 1965, he was reassigned to work in a lime quarry but forbidden to wear sunglasses. The glare from the lime permanently damaged his eyesight.

Classified as the lowest grade of prisoner, Class D, he was allowed just one heavily censored letter and one personal visit every six months. Newspapers were forbidden and he was locked in solitary confinement on many occasions for possessing smuggled news clippings.

When he was finally released from prison in 1990, he didn't call for revenge but for forgiveness and reconciliation among his countrymen. He said, "Men of peace must not think about retribution or recriminations. Courageous people do not fear forgiving, for the sake of peace." He resumed his leadership role with the African National Congress, and in 1994, he was elected as the first black president of South Africa. At his inauguration, Nelson Mandela kept a seat set aside for a special guest as a show of national reconciliation: one of his white jailers during his imprisonment at Robben Island.

Forgiveness not only freed Nelson Mandela, it also changed the course of history for South Africa. His fellow citizens were so inspired by Mandela's forgiveness that they also sought reconciliation for the good of their country, and the world took notice. He became one of the most decorated and respected political leaders in the history of the world. This is what is possible when we forgive our way to freedom. Perhaps your reconciliation won't be earth-shattering; perhaps the world won't take notice. But God will. And that's cause enough to celebrate.

So let me close this chapter with three questions: (1) Is there someone you need to forgive and reconcile with? (2) Is there someone you need to ask for forgiveness so you can be reconciled? (3) What on earth are you waiting for?

Forgiveness Prayer

Heavenly Father, I'm so grateful that You gave Your Son, Jesus, to forgive my sins and to make reconciliation possible with You. Give me the courage and the loving words to approach those who have sinned against me in hopes we can restore our relationship. Reveal to me anyone whom I have sinned against so I may repent to that person and be reconciled.

Reflect and Discuss

1. What did you think of the inscription on the tombstone that I mentioned at the beginning of this chapter?
2. Have you made an issue more important than a relationship?
3. Why should the person who's been hurt initiate reconciliation?
4. Have you tried to reconcile with someone but they weren't willing? What do you think you should do next?

Your Turn: Apply What You're Learning

Be patient as reconciling may require more than one attempt. Keep trying if you value this relationship. Like the father of the prodigal son in the story, keep looking, keep hoping, and always be ready when the time comes. If this person refuses to reconcile, then you are free. It is now between this person and God.

CHAPTER 11

Forgive Yourself and Make Peace with God

"There is now no condemnation for those who are in Christ Jesus."

THE APOSTLE PAUL, in Romans 8:1

L ate on the evening of Thanksgiving 1980 I received a phone call from my older brother Jim. He was calling with terrible news that our twenty-two-year-old brother, Freddie, had ingested arsenic poison in an attempt to commit suicide.

Freddie had long struggled with depression, and the recent breakup of his marriage had apparently pushed him over the edge. He had been rushed to the hospital, where he now battled for his life with tubes running in and out of his body. My other brothers and sisters were arriving on the scene, but I was three hours away and at a loss about what to do. I was feeling numb from the news and found it difficult to think.

I recalled the time when my sister was about two years old and accidentally swallowed toxic kitchen cleaner. She was rushed to the hospital, where the doctors pumped her stomach, and she survived the ordeal. In my desperate attempt to cling to a positive outlook, I thought perhaps this would be the case with Freddie. He was in good hands, there were plenty of family members around, and so I decided not to go. Jim promised to keep me informed of any news throughout the night.

I immediately began to pray, but I found it difficult since I had never been confronted with anything like this before. I kept picturing Freddie's face in my mind as I prayed for God to spare his life. I was sure Freddie would survive the night. And once he did, I would have a second chance to tell him how much I loved him and to make sure this would never happen again.

After I prayed, I lay back in bed and continued to think about Freddie. He was just eighteen months younger than me. Since there were eleven kids in our family, Freddie and I shared a bed growing up. Brothers share many secrets and dreams when they have to sleep in the same bed for so many years. We probably knew each other better than anyone else. And we were inseparable during the days too, though not by my choice. Freddie followed me everywhere despite my best efforts to shake him off. He imitated me constantly. He irritated me relentlessly. When I complained to Mom that he hounded me all the time, she always said, "It's because he loves you."

Freddie didn't have many friends of his own during our childhood, so he mostly hung out with me and my friends. He may have loved following me around and constantly bugging me, but he paid a heavy price for my ruthless disposition as his big brother. I was considerably larger than him. He was a peace-loving kid while I always had an attitude. Consequently, he became my punching bag and the recipient of countless insults and abuse as we were growing up.

Ironically, I never tolerated anyone else picking on Freddie. We had it pretty rough as kids, especially fitting in at school. We were really poor and didn't have nice clothes, plus we were a very religious family. We were bullied mercilessly for being poor and different. Freddie and I were in Cub Scouts for about six months. We were the only kids in the entire pack who couldn't afford uniforms. We both grew so weary of the constant taunting that we finally dropped out.

Since I had an attitude, I fought back when kids picked on me, but not Freddie. He never fought back. I had a growth spurt in grade school and outgrew many of the bullies. So I appointed myself his protector and made it clear that anyone who picked on my little brother would have to answer to me. Most of the fights I had in school and most of the visits to the principal's office were because I was defending Freddie.

Now that we were both grown, I wanted more opportunities to connect with my little brother as men. During my previous visit to St. Louis, we had enjoyed a great time together. We talked and laughed a lot and even got in a quick game of basketball before I departed. He trash-talked me the whole time for being so out of shape, and I had to prove that Big Brother could still take him down. Now here he was fighting for his life, and there was nothing I could do.

The phone rang at six o'clock the next morning. It was my brother Jim and he said just two words: *He's gone.* Those words still echo in my mind after all these years. Jim's voice was little more than a whisper. He explained that the doctors had worked tirelessly to save Freddie but there was too much poison in his system. The last thing Freddie told Jim before he slipped away was that he had made things right with God and he was ready to meet Jesus. That truth offered comfort, but in that terrible moment, all I could focus on was that my little brother had committed suicide. I wasn't there when he needed me most and I wasn't there when he died. Why hadn't I gone that night?

For the next several years, I returned to Freddie's grave on the anniversary of his death. I always went alone and I repeated the same ritual. As I stood by his tombstone, I reminisced about our relationship. I recalled how much I had resented him when we were kids. I remembered all the times I had picked on him and said hurtful things to him. I questioned why I hadn't known he was suicidal. And of course, I remembered with shame how I chose not to drive to the hospital the night he died.

The same grace I was so willing to give everyone else was something I thought I never deserved.

I never got to say goodbye or tell him how much I loved him. Within minutes I would drop to my knees at his grave and weep uncontrollably. Over and over I'd cry, "Freddie, I'm so sorry. I'm so sorry." After wiping away my tears, I would look up into the cold November sky and voice the same prayer: "Jesus, the next time You see Freddie, please tell him I am so sorry." Then I'd leave feeling so empty inside with no resolution to my pain.

After about twenty-five years of this misery, a turning point came the year my wife, Patricia, went with me to visit Freddie's grave. She had always honored my desire to go alone, but we were in the area and I thought it was time that she came with me to the cemetery. As we stood together at Freddie's gravesite on this day, I intuitively went into my annual routine of weeping and begging forgiveness. Having never accompanied me before, Patricia was surprised to see these wounds so fresh after so many years. Quietly, Patricia knelt beside me and put her arm around me as I continued to mourn. She then whispered one of the most liberating truths I have ever heard: "Sweetheart, Freddie forgave you a long time ago. You have never forgiven yourself. It's time for you to lay that burden down."

As someone who has studied and taught on forgivness for

decades, I'm embarrassed to share what I'm about to admit to you now. After so many years of anguish, it never occurred to me to forgive myself. I had been privileged to help so many other people forgive their way to freedom, yet here I was unable to do the same for myself. The same grace I was so willing to give everyone else was something I thought I never deserved.

And so right there at Freddie's grave, I forgave my way to freedom. I literally spoke these words out loud, "Gil, I forgive you. I forgive you for not being a better brother to Freddie. I forgive you for all the hurtful things you said and did to Freddie. I forgive you, Gil, for the pain and disappointment you caused. And I forgive you for not being there when Freddie died." In that moment, years of guilt lifted and I was free! I no longer needed to ask Jesus to tell Freddie I was sorry. In fact, I believe Jesus and Freddie were looking down and celebrating that precious moment with me.

Have You Forgiven Yourself?

Often the hardest person we have to forgive is ourselves. If you've ever been a serious victim, you have likely felt devalued or shamed as a person, and you may think you are unworthy of love or forgiveness. Like me, you find it much easier to extend grace to others but you refuse to give yourself that same grace. You may be struggling with mistakes, bad choices, or hurtful things you have done in the past and are struggling to forgive yourself.

The Bible doesn't explicitly talk about forgiving ourselves. However, the principles of forgiveness also apply to us. We must seek to resolve the pain resulting from our own mistakes, working to restore our peace and reclaiming our purpose for the future.

In addition to forgiving ourselves, the principles of loving ourselves also apply to us. First Corinthians 13:4–8 gives us a beautiful description of the kind of love we should show to others. But we need to extend this same love toward ourselves.

A powerful way I've found to do this is to pray this passage of Scripture, inserting my own name:

Gil is patient with himself. Gil is kind to himself. Because Gil is so loved, he is not jealous or boastful or proud. Gil is not rude to others and he doesn't demand his own way. Gil is not easily angered. Gil keeps no record of wrongs. Gil does not delight in evil, but he rejoices with the truth. Gil never gives up, never loses faith, is always hopeful, and endures through every circumstance.

Try this for yourself. Don't just recite it—believe it! Then as we look outward to resolve the pain of the past, we must also look inward. Don't repeat my mistake. Don't refuse to forgive yourself because you don't see what is so obvious right in front of you.

I love the riddle that asks, "What do you use to sit on, sleep on, and brush your teeth?" It's funny to watch people rack their brains trying to solve the riddle, but it is especially amusing when I tell them the answer: a chair, a bed, and a toothbrush. Yep, we often look past the obvious and make things more complicated than they need to be. When you reach out to forgive others, don't look past the most obvious person of all: yourself.

If we don't forgive ourselves, we're saying that Jesus Christ's shed blood and sacrificial death on the cross is not enough. It is enough for God. It is enough for everyone else. And yes, my friend, it is more than enough for you to forgive yourself.

Forgiving God?

As we work to forgive our way to freedom, it's also important to carefully evaluate how our forgiveness journey has affected our relationship with God. Has your experience drawn you closer or pushed you further away from God? Do you hold Him responsible for any of your painful past? Is there anything you need to clear up between you and God? As strange as this may sound, do you feel the need to forgive God?

I've never found any reference in the Bible where God needed to be forgiven. If I truly believe God loves me and that He is holy and perfect, it is impossible for me to believe that He would do anything against me that would require my forgiveness. I don't think it is ever wrong to question God. It is when we blame God that we drive ourselves from Him.

The story of Job is about a man who lost everything. In one day, he lost all his children, all his livestock, all his servants, and all his wealth. Instead of blaming God and becoming angry with Him, Job's response was, "'Naked I came from my mother's womb, and naked I will depart. The LORD gave and the LORD has taken away; may the name of the LORD be praised.' *In all this, Job did not sin by charging God with wrongdoing*" (Job 1:21–22).

Making peace with God is not about forgiving Him. Instead, it's about reconciling with Him for how we may have blamed Him or held God responsible for our troubles. Instead of demanding that God conform to our finite understanding of how life should work or feeling betrayed when He has not granted our every desire or wish, we need to repent for our doubts, anger, pride, stubbornness, distrust, and lack of faith.

God not only encourages faith, He requires it. The Bible teaches, "It is by grace you have been saved, through faith" (Eph. 2:8). In fact, the Bible makes it clear that faith is essential when it comes to God: "Without faith it is impossible to please God, because anyone who comes to him must believe that he exists and that he rewards those who earnestly seek him" (Heb. 11:6). And it is through faith that we can find peace with God: "Since we have been justified through faith, we have peace with God through our Lord Jesus Christ" (Rom. 5:1).

Trust Is the Pathway to Peace

It's tough, if not impossible, to answer why evil exists, why bad things happen to good people, or why some prayers appear to get answered while others don't. I can choose to spend my life in bitter disappointment and second-guessing why the omnipotent and omniscient God of the universe has not performed according to my human expectations, but that would only make me more bitter. I can choose to spend my life blaming God for my choices or other people's choices, but that will never bring me resolution or freedom.

The alternative is that I can choose to trust that God has a depth of understanding that I can never grasp, and that He has a love for me that I cannot begin to comprehend. Simply put, I can accept the truth that God is smarter than I am, and if He created me and gave His Son, Jesus, to die for me, He must have a plan for my life. The wisest man who ever lived urged us all to "trust in the LORD with all your heart and lean not on your own understanding" (Prov. 3:5).

When you reach out to forgive others, don't look past the most obvious person of all: yourself.

Trusting God means believing that He sometimes allows suffering to accomplish a greater purpose, much like gold is purified when it's tested by fire. When we trust God, the pain, disappointments, and circumstances that could have destroyed us are instead woven into a beautiful tapestry that makes us who we are.

The depth of our love, the measure of our compassion, the extent of our wisdom, the joy of our gratitude, our capacity to forgive, and our personal walk with the Lord are all forged by faith through things we don't entirely understand but choose to entrust to God. But will we wait until we see how things turn out before we trust God or will we take the step of faith to trust Him now, in the midst of our troubling circumstances?

Consider again Job and all the tragic losses he endured. We could all understand if Job had some serious questions for the Almighty. Near the end of his book, in chapter 38, God responds to Job's questions with His own questions:

> Where were you when I laid the earth's foundation?
>
> Who commands the morning to come or the sun where to rise?
>
> Where does the light and the darkness come from?
>
> Who tells the rain where it should fall or makes paths for the thunderstorms?
>
> Do you know the laws that govern the heavens or rule the earth?[1]

After hearing God's series of rhetorical questions, Job responds in the last chapter by saying, "I spoke of things I did not understand, things too wonderful for me to know" (Job 42:3). Job learned to trust God and his life completely turned around. In fact, "The LORD blessed the latter part of Job's life more than the former part" (Job 42:12). We cannot answer all of life's hard questions, and we may not have control over what happens to us at all times, but we have 100 percent control when it comes to trusting God, which is the pathway to peace and freedom. Trusting God is not just believing despite the circumstances but obeying regardless of the consequences.

Ultimately, forgiveness is all about trusting God. If you've never experienced God's forgiveness for your sins, I'd love to invite you to do that right now. The first step to eternity with God begins with forgiveness. It's also the reason Jesus died on the cross. But it's about so much more than everlasting life in heaven.

Jesus also came to give our lives joy, fulfillment, and purpose. This amazing offer is not something we deserve and it's not something we can earn by being "good enough." It's a free gift for everyone. Inviting Jesus into your life is as simple as A–B–C. Here are some Bible verses you can look up on your own.

> A— ADMIT to God that you are a sinner. Nobody's perfect. We all need forgiveness. (See John 3:16, Acts 3:19; Rom. 3:23; Rom. 6:23; 1 John 1:9.)
>
> B— BELIEVE that Jesus is God's Son and accept God's gift of forgiveness from your sin. (See John 14:6; Acts 4:12; Rom. 5:8; Eph. 2:8–9.)
>
> C— CONFESS your faith in Jesus Christ as your Savior and Lord. (See Rom. 10:9–10, 13.)

If you're ready to become a Christian, here's a prayer to help get you started:

> Dear God, I know I have sinned and that my sin separates me from You. I am sorry for my sin. I believe Jesus died on the cross so my sins can be forgiven. God, please forgive me. I ask Jesus to come into my life and be my Savior and Lord, and I will live for You the rest of my life. Amen.

Now that you've repented and received God's forgiveness, what are the next steps?

1. Tell someone about your decision.
2. Start reading the Bible beginning with the book of John in an easy translation, such as the New International Version or the paraphrased Living Bible.

3. Find a church in your area to attend that clearly teaches the Bible and seek to be baptized.
4. Grow in God's grace as you continue to apply yourself to His plan for your life.
5. Keep talking to God in prayer. He would love to hear from you and be your heavenly Father for the rest of your life and into eternity.

As you are now equipped to reconcile broken relationships, including forgiving yourself, and you've made things right with God, you're free to focus on a bright, new future. Look out world, here you come!

Forgiveness Prayer

Dear Lord, thank You that I can ask You hard questions when I don't understand and that You forgive me when I doubt You. I want to replace my temptation to blame You and others with a mindset of gratitude because I know all things are working together for my good. I also know that forgiveness includes myself, which I will do now and going forward. Thank You most of all for saving my soul through Your forgiveness to me.

Reflect and Discuss

1. Can you think of a time when you struggled to forgive yourself?
2. Do you give yourself the same grace you give to others? If not, why not?

3. Was there ever a time when you blamed God for
   something? Why? How do you feel about that
   now?
4. How much do you trust God? What would
   make you trust Him more?

Your Turn: Apply What You've Learned

Take a serious examination of your life to see if you've
fully forgiven yourself. Ask a trusted friend or family
member to give you their perspective. And talk to God
about any times you blamed Him for something. Open
your Bible to 1 Corinthians 13 and insert your name
before each definition of love. This is how God loves you
and wants you to love yourself.

CHAPTER 12

Your Fate Is Not Your Destiny

"It's never too late to be what you might have been."

GEORGE ELIOT

With a proper understanding of forgiveness, we are able to unleash our power, as we discussed at the beginning of this book. Once we have done that, we can begin to look back to move forward and resolve our past pain. This empowers us to "let go and let God" to experience freedom now. We are now free to rediscover our purpose and hope! As the Bible encourages, "Let us throw off everything that hinders and the sin that so easily entangles. And let us run with perseverance the race marked out for us" (Heb. 12:1).

God has a special purpose for you, which only you can fulfill. The Bible says, "Before I formed you in the womb I knew you, before you were born I set you apart" (Jer. 1:5). God was meticulous when He created the breathtaking landscapes of earth and the majestic stars of the universe, but you are His masterpiece. He created you, redeemed you, gifted you, and envisioned an amazing plan for your life. As Paul reminds us, "We are God's handiwork, created in Christ Jesus to do good works, which God prepared in advance for us to do" (Eph. 2:10)

To measure our value in God's eyes, consider the fact that

He gave His only Son, Jesus, to die for our sins. "He who did not spare his own Son, but gave him up for us all—how will he not also, along with him, graciously give us all things?" (Rom. 8:32). God didn't just give us Jesus to escape hell so we can spend eternity in heaven. He also wants us to experience an abundant, fulfilling life here and now (see John 10:10).

But God's purpose for us sometimes gets derailed. Most often it is because of our sin when we willfully disobey Him. Our sin hinders our prayers, kills our joy, robs our peace, poisons our soul, and breaks our fellowship with God. In addition, our sin neutralizes God's purpose in our lives. His Spirit is grieved when we settle for so much less than what He wants for us.

Other things can foil God's purpose for our lives, such as being too busy with smaller things or too fearful to try new things. However, nothing knocks us off track quite like unforgiveness. All of us have a destiny, but some never achieve it because a hurtful incident in their past has clipped their wings and they cannot soar as God intended. I'm referring to this as "fate," which are those unavoidable circumstances that are often beyond our control. Many resign to their fate and can waste their lives in bitterness and anger. But while we may not have had a choice in the fate life may have chosen for us, we do have a choice in overcoming our fate to the destiny that *God* has chosen for us. Whatever your fate, it does not have to be your destiny.

Stepping Out into Destiny

If fate had ever been unkind to anyone, it was Bart Millard.

Bart's father, Arthur Wesley Millard Jr., was a local high school football hero and one of only two All-Americans from the small town of Greenville, Texas. His life was going well until he was hit by a diesel truck, which put him in a coma for eight weeks. When he woke up, he was a different man. The loving man known as

"Bub" became mean, angry, and bitter. Three years later, Bart was born into a home full of tension. And when Bart was three years old, his parents divorced.

Bart lived with his mother at first, but he and his older brother had to move back with their dad when his mother moved out of town with her third husband. Tensions arose when Bart's dad would give his brother and him spankings. Soon these spankings turned into four or five beatings every week for things that had nothing to do with the children's behavior. They were the punching bag for their father's constant rage.

When the beatings finally stopped, they were replaced with total apathy from his dad, who made it clear he didn't care about Bart. For Bart, his father's emotional abandonment hurt more than the beatings. When Bart tried to make his dad proud, he was met with more apathy and even mocking.

Bart clung to his faith in God and his desire to be a professional singer, even though his dad often ridiculed him over them. And then his dad received a massive wake-up call: cancer. His dad would live only four years after his diagnosis.

During those last four years, God did an amazing work in Bart's father. He began attending church and became a Christian. The change was so dramatic that Bart found it hard to believe. He felt that God may forgive his dad for all he had done with his abuse, but Bart wasn't ready to forgive. It took time for Bart to eventually come around and forgive his own way to freedom. And in the final years, Bart and his father became so close that when his father died, Bart was actually upset with God because he had finally gotten the dad he'd always wanted, only to lose him to death.

At his father's gravesite, Bart's grandmother said, "I can only imagine what Bub's seeing now." Those words echoed in Bart's mind for years until he finally wrote his thoughts in a song he called, "I Can Only Imagine."[1]

After years of abuse and abandonment from his father and constant rejection from the music industry, his simple song would touch millions of lives and become the bestselling Christian single of all time, and the first Christian song in history to be certified triple platinum by the Recording Industry Association of America. And recently his story was turned into a movie, *I Can Only Imagine*, which will inspire millions more.

For Bart Millard, his fate was not his destiny. But none of this success and outreach would have happened if he hadn't forgiven his way to freedom. Instead of living out his life in bitterness and blaming his abusive father, Bart chose to forgive his father to reclaim his purpose. This same wonderful hope is available to you too. Whatever challenges fate may have given you, it is not your destiny.

Consider the words of Booker T. Washington, one of the last generation of black American leaders born into slavery. He went on to become an accomplished educator, author, orator, and advisor to US presidents. Between 1890 and 1915, Washington was the dominant leader in the black community in America. He wrote in his book *Up From Slavery*: "Success is to be measured not so much by the position that one has reached in life as by the obstacles which he has overcome."[2] If anyone knew about rising up from a painful past to forgive his way to freedom, it was Booker T. Washington.

In the previous chapter, we discussed how God has created each of us with a purpose, with dreams, and a call to fulfill. And for each of us, as life gets in the way, we must decide how we will respond. We can allow what others have done to us to dictate our destiny. Or we can push forward, forgive the wounds of the past, and use what we've learned to lead us to achieve our God-given destiny.

To offer another example: most professional baseball players can easily hit a fastball because it comes straight down the middle of the strike zone. But the great players are ones who can also hit a curveball, which twists and turns on its way to home plate. So it is with life. Anyone can flourish under the best of circumstances, but the truly great ones are those who can overcome the curveballs of life to reclaim their purpose.

Life may have thrown you a nasty curveball or two that you didn't see coming and has veered you off course. You may have settled for so much less than God's perfect plan for your life because your wounds have left you afraid to fully live again. You may have become resigned to your fate as though the story of your life has already been written. The psalmist has a different perspective about God's plan: "Your eyes saw my unformed body; all the days ordained for me were written in your book before one of them came to be" (Ps. 139:16).

But things happen that slow us down or stop us altogether. Harboring bitterness, trying to control other people's actions, or refusing to forgive can prolong our recovery. We need to grieve our losses, resolve our pain, and restore our peace. And at some point we find ourselves at a crossroads toward our future. Will we continue to live in the past like helpless victims or will we choose instead to venture into a bold new future where God is waiting and the angels are cheering?

I love the song "I Will Listen" by Twila Paris. One line from those lyrics asks, "Could it be that He is only waiting there to see if I will learn to love the dreams that He has dreamed for me?" While we've been waiting for God to move us on toward our purpose, it is God who has been waiting for us the whole time. Now that we've forgiven, we are free to embrace our purpose!

Dare to Dream Again

One of my greatest Bible heroes is Joseph from the book of Genesis. Joseph was a dreamer. His dreams were visions of grandeur, with him as the ruler over his family. He was already the favored son of Jacob, who honored him with a colorful coat that made him the envy of his brothers. So with his father's love and God's blessings, Joseph was destined for greatness. But enraged by their father's special treatment of Joseph, his jealous brothers sold him into slavery in Egypt. What a devastating blow for young Joseph.

More than a decade passed as Joseph served as a slave to one of the pharaoh's officials named Potiphar. This fate was surely not what Joseph had dreamed and yet he accepted it and remained true to his faith. God blessed Joseph despite his limitations as a slave, and Potiphar took notice. He put Joseph in charge of his entire household, and all that Joseph did prospered. But soon once again, cruel fate intervened when Potiphar's wife tried to seduce him. When he refused her advances, she falsely accused him. Now Joseph was thrown in prison for a crime he did not commit.

This was the favored son of Jacob, the dreamer of great things, the dreamer with the brightly colored coat. He had been thrown in a pit, sold as a slave, worked more than a decade proving himself to Potiphar, and now he was in prison for a crime he didn't commit. From all outward appearances, his destiny had been ruined by his fate.

More years passed. Joseph was now in his thirties, and it appeared that life had killed the dreams he dreamed. But someone else was dreaming—literally. The mighty Pharaoh had a dream and desperately needed an interpretation. Joseph was the only one in Egypt who could help Pharoah. And for his service, Joseph was promoted to second in command of all of Egypt. Because of Joseph's unshakable faithfulness to God, fate was at last giving way to destiny.

He could move on and forgive those who had harmed him because he was, by all accounts, successful. Joseph had now been in Egypt more than twenty years, and just when things couldn't be going better for him, *they showed up.* The same brothers who sold him as a slave arrived in Egypt to buy grain during a terrible drought. He was faced with a decision about truly resolving his past, letting it go, and forgiving so that he could live freely.

Through a series of events, he revealed to his brothers his true identity. They were sure he would seek vengeance and now turn them into slaves or worse. Though fully justified to retaliate for all they had put him through, Joseph made a different choice: forgiveness.[3]

If you have struggled with forgiveness, think of how much time and energy you wasted that you can now invest into a healthy and exciting future.

Joseph's choice to forgive did more than help him survive when fate turned against him over and over again. His forgiveness did more than restore his family. His act of forgiveness saved Israel, the people from which Jesus would one day come. In short, Joseph's forgiveness changed the world. *That* was his true destiny!

Much like Joseph, you may have been destined for a different purpose but found yourself in a pit. You may have felt as though you were a slave to someone else's choices or your own actions. Even when you tried to do right, like Joseph, you were mistreated and misunderstood. However, I pray you will follow Joseph's example and not accept your fate as your destiny.

God revealed to Joseph at an early age that He had a purpose for his life. Even as he suffered innocently in an Egyptian prison for years, Joseph never lost sight of God's purpose or His promises. He chose not to waste those years in bitterness, anger, and unforgiveness toward his brothers but to focus on God's purpose. You and I have that same power today.

If you have struggled with forgiveness, think of how much time and energy you wasted that you can now invest into a healthy and exciting future. You have stepped out of your self-made jail cell and into the sunlight where joy, peace, and victory await you. That big boulder that was once in the road and preventing you from moving forward has now been pushed aside, and you are free to proceed with the rest of your life.

God is all about freedom. Paul tells us, "Now the Lord is the Spirit, and where the Spirit of the Lord is, there is freedom" (2 Cor. 3:17). He has always wanted you to be free because He has so much more for you. He has been patiently and lovingly waiting for you, and now that you're ready, God is eager to take you to the next level to enjoy the fruits of freedom.

Beauty from Brokenness

When something we love gets broken beyond repair, we see it as useless and sadly throw it in the trash. We can also see our lives as broken, and from these setbacks, we lose sight of our God-given purpose. Things did not go the way we planned, and we may think that our hopes and dreams are no longer attainable. But we need to understand that we can reclaim our purpose not in spite of our brokenness, but *because* of it.

Kintsugi is an ancient Japanese art, which means "golden repair." According to legend, Japanese shogun Ashikaga Yoshimasa had his prized tea bowl fall and break into pieces. Heartbroken, he had it sent to China for repair, but when he received it back, he was displeased with the workmanship because it was mended using cheap metal staples. So he took the bowl to a Japanese craftsman who sealed the pieces back together and inlayed each crack with solid gold. The cracked tea bowl was not just lined with precious gold, but because of the randomness of its cracks, it was the only one of its kind in all the world, which made it priceless. Artisans from all over Japan began breaking tea bowls on purpose to create these masterpieces, and the art of kintsugi was born.[4]

Many of us were once like that broken tea bowl that was shattered and appeared useless. However, God has lovingly pieced us together to create a true masterpiece! We have this wonderful promise from God: "I will put beautiful crowns on their heads in place of ashes. I will anoint them with olive oil to give them joy instead of sorrow. I will give them a spirit of praise in place of a spirit of sadness" (Isa. 61:3 NIrv).

And just like the uniqueness of each broken vessel, there is no one like you in all the world! God doesn't want you to be like someone He has already created. He wants you to be the exquisite work of art and genius He created you to be. By embracing forgiveness, you can reclaim your purpose. Have you ever considered that those things in your life that once created so much sorrow can now work for you to make you better than if you hadn't gone through those experiences?

Will you continue to live in the past like a helpless victim or will you choose to venture into a bold new future where God is waiting?

God does not cause our pain but He is also not taken by surprise when bad things happen. God never says, "Oops, I didn't see that coming." But God can weave every heartache, every setback, every disappointment, and every tear in an amazing patchwork, which makes us who we are so we can fulfill our purpose. His Word says, "We can rejoice, too, when we run into problems and trials, for we know that they are good for us—they help us learn to be patient. And patience develops strength of character in us and helps us trust God more each time we use it until finally our hope and faith are strong and steady" (Rom. 5:3–4 TLB).

My precious friend, there's nothing you've ever done that God cannot forgive, and there's nothing that has ever happened to you that God cannot redeem. Throughout this book I have shared true stories of forgiveness, reconciliation, and redemption. I purposely did not offer sugarcoated stories about perfect saints but real people with real problems. In every case, starting with my own story, they overcame incredible obstacles and forgave their way to freedom. Think about this: if I hadn't gone through my own painful past, you wouldn't be reading this book right now!

It's time for you to get off the bench on the sideline of life and get back in the game. Go back to your original goals, or create new ones. Starting today, you can unleash the power that's always been inside you. Trust me, the world needs more good forgivers like you!

Leaving a Legacy of Forgiveness

One of the turning points in the history of the Christian faith was the martyrdom of Stephen, which is recorded in the early chapters of the book of Acts. Most people are surprised to learn that more people have been killed for their Christian faith in the last century than all previous centuries combined, but Stephen was the first.

As the early church was growing into the thousands, Stephen was one of seven leaders chosen and commissioned by the apostles for his remarkable reputation, his godly wisdom, and because he was full of the Holy Spirit. His role as a deacon was to serve the poor and needy so the apostles could devote themselves to teaching and to praying.

He was outspoken about the new Christian faith that posed such a threat to the religious establishment at the time. As opposition arose, Stephen surfaced as a spokesperson and proved to be a skilled debater against those who challenged the followers of Christ. Acts 6:10 says, "They could not stand up against the wisdom the Spirit gave him as he spoke." This infuriated the ruling religious class, and so they resorted to the age-old tactic still employed today when you're losing the argument—you assassinate the person's character.

Vicious lies were created to discredit Stephen, and the leaders took him before the religious council to stand trial for his alleged blasphemy. Despite a passionate and truthful defense, an angry crowd that had gathered to witness this mockery of justice literally covered their ears and shouted him down. The mob grabbed Stephen and dragged him outside the city gates of Jerusalem to administer their perverted justice as self-imposed judges and executioners. He was then stoned to death.

To this day stoning remains one of the most brutal and barbaric forms of capital punishment. It is nothing more than a group of rabble-rousers throwing stones at the accused. Those hurling the rocks are careful not to aim at the head, lest it render the accused unconscious prematurely. The goal is for this poor soul to feel the full pain of the rocks breaking bones, piercing flesh, and spilling blood before passing out and succumbing to death. A "proper" stoning takes about twenty minutes.

It was as this horrible scene was playing out that Stephen offered this prayer of forgiveness as his final words: "Lord! Don't hold this sin against them!" (Acts 7:60 nirv).

The remarkable thing is that this display of grace did not appear to make any difference to the crowd. They kept throwing their rocks. When Jesus once stood before such an angry mob who wanted to stone a woman caught in adultery, He challenged the one without sin to cast the first stone. The crowd dispersed (see John 8:2–11).

Here was a man extending forgiveness to the very people who were murdering him—and they killed him anyway! It appeared that evil had triumphed over good, and that Stephen's godly life, his righteous stand for truth, his martyr's death, and his amazing prayer of forgiveness made absolutely no difference.

Now let's turn our attention to the apostle Paul. There was

a man who did make a difference. Unlike Stephen, whose light was snuffed out quickly and unceremoniously, Paul was the most influential force for the Christian cause in history. We easily see the difference he made in his dynamic preaching, his powerful writings, his vast church planting, and his exciting missionary journeys. But it is not coincidental that the first mention in the Bible of the great apostle Paul was at Stephen's stoning.

It's easy to miss. It almost seems out of place. He was little more than a bystander as the mob murdered Stephen. The Bible mentions in passing that "the witnesses laid their coats at the feet of a young man named Saul" (Acts 7:58). On the day Stephen was being stoned for his courageous stand for Christ, this young man witnessed the whole thing.

We know this same Saul would one day meet the resurrected Christ on the road to Damascus and change his name to Paul. After his miraculous conversion, he would go into the desert for three years to relearn all he had been taught from his religious orientation. He would come back to Jerusalem one day to eventually be embraced by the early Christians and rise to become the great apostle.

But I've often wondered how much of an impact the death of Stephen had on Paul's conversion when he witnessed a godly man look his murderers in the eyes and say, "I forgive you." Could this scene have kept him awake at night or convicted him about his own need for forgiveness? This may just be my opinion, but I believe it was Stephen's amazing expression of forgiveness that began to change this man who would one day change the whole world!

Paul would go on to say, "Pass on to people you can trust the things you've heard me say. Then they will be able to teach others also" (2 Tim. 2:2 NIrv). His destiny was to help others find their way to freedom in Christ. All because of forgiveness. Now that you have forgiven your way to freedom, just as Paul encouraged his listeners, you need to teach others about forgiveness.

First and foremost, we need to tell others about God's forgiveness of their sins through the death of His Son, Jesus Christ, and how they can be completely reconciled to God and spend eternity in heaven. Next, we need to model for them what forgiveness looks like in our own lives. Last, we need them to forgive *their* way to freedom.

Thank you for the honor of being your temporary tour guide through this process. Though we've walked through some hard and painful stuff to find our freedom, I'm comforted that the day will come when God Himself will wipe away the tears from our eyes (see Rev. 21:4). Until that great and final day, my prayer is for you:

For all you have yet to see, God will show you.
For all you have yet to learn, God will teach you.
And for all you have yet to become, God will make you.
Enjoy your freedom!

Forgiveness Prayer

Dear God, You are the One who makes all things new. Thank You that You have a purpose for my life. I want to commit myself to fulfilling that purpose. I want to be the best me You created. May I never allow unforgiveness to stand in the way. May I begin even now to overcome my fate to fulfil my destiny!

Reflect and Discuss

1. When have you felt resigned to your fate? What helped you move on?
2. In what ways have you rediscovered God's purpose for your life?
3. If you could do *anything* you wanted to going forward, what would it be?
4. What steps will you take, starting today, to make that dream come true?

Your Turn: Apply What You're Learning

Go back to the Forgiveness Evaluation in the appendix and retake the test. You may not get a perfect score, but celebrate your progress and keep forgiving your way to freedom.

Forgiveness Questionnaire and Evaluation

This evaluation will help you determine how well you're progressing on your road to forgiving your way to freedom. Read through the list of statements below and carefully note if each one is TRUE or FALSE for you. After you take it yourself, you might consider inviting a trusted friend or family member to answer the same questions about you to get a more objective perspective.

To get the best sense of your journey and to best measure your progress, I encourage you to take this evaluation before you read the book and then again after you have completed the book. Be honest with yourself, but also give yourself grace as you improve. Remember, forgiveness is a process.

1. I don't have any friends or family who have told me I need to forgive someone else.
2. I can think of my offender without negative feelings of stress, anger, or bitterness.
3. I do not keep track of ways that other people have hurt me.
4. I do not say bad things about those who have caused me pain.
5. I don't share my story of hurt or betrayal repeatedly to other people.

6. When I'm in public I do not go out of my way to avoid the person who hurt me.

7. It would not be uncomfortable to talk to this person face-to-face.

8. I can be completely objective about my experience, despite my painful past.

9. I have no doubts about my self-worth regardless of what happened to me.

10. I never think of ways I'd like to get revenge against people who hurt me.

11. I can be happy for my offender if they succeed and do well.

12. I do not struggle to accept and receive love from other people or my family.

13. I easily forgive myself when I make poor decisions that impact my life.

14. I do not need addictive behaviors to cover up or escape from my pain.

15. I don't have difficulty expressing myself or telling people how I feel.

16. I do not have a problem trying to please other people.

17. I do not let people take advantage of me.

18. I do not let what other people think of me determine my value.

19. I can usually embrace the truth, even when a lie "feels" true.

20. I don't compare myself with other people and I don't feel that my life is unfair.

21. I do not blame others for the problems in my life.

22. I don't believe my health has been affected by my struggle to forgive.

23. I have learned new insights that have helped me by recounting my pain in my mind.
24. I am as close to God today as when I first began trying to forgive my offender.
25. I am experiencing freedom through forgiveness.

YOUR SCORE

0–4 FALSE: Congratulations, you're doing very well. Hopefully this will help you identify some areas where you may need to work. Even if you feel that forgiveness may not be a strong issue for you, it's likely that you may know someone else who is struggling and would benefit from this teaching.

5–9 FALSE: This would be a clear indication that you are working through some forgiveness issues that have yet to be resolved. Be encouraged! This book will help you find the freedom that you seek and deserve.

10–14 FALSE: Forgiveness is a very definite issue for you, and your struggle is keeping you from the joy and peace God wants for your life. The good news is that this book was written with you in mind. Inside you will find the tools you need so you can experience the full joy, power, and freedom of forgiveness.

15+ FALSE: At this point you may want to seriously consider professional counseling to help, you manage your trauma. This book will help, but it is not intended to replace the therapy you may need from a qualified counselor.

Resources for Victims of Abuse

The National Domestic Violence Hotline
1-800-799-SAFE
Trained advocates are available 24/7 to talk confidentially with anyone experiencing domestic violence, seeking resources or information, or questioning unhealthy aspects of their relationship.

The National Sexual Assault Hotline
1-800-656-HOPE
Call 24/7 to be connected with a trained staff member from a sexual assault service provider in your area.

The Childhelp National Child Abuse Hotline
1-800-4-A-CHILD (422-4453)
The hotline is staffed 24 hours a day, 7 days a week with professional crisis counselors who offer intervention, information, and referrals to thousands of emergency, social services, and support resources.

FOCUS Ministries
1-630-617-0088
https://www.focusministries1.org
Focus offers faith-based domestic violence help for women and families.

The Mend Project
http://themendproject.com
This is not a crisis center, but they provide excellent resources to help educate, equip, and restore victims of abuse, their partners, and counselors.

Notes

How Good a Forgiver Are You?

1. "Bitterness and Forgiveness," The Children's Bread, December 2, 2016, http://the childrensbread.org/getting-free/bitterness-forgiveness/.
2. See John 8:32.

Chapter 2: The Top Ten Myths of Forgiveness

1. Dictionary.com, Complacency, http://www.dictionary.com/browse/complacency?s=t.
2. Johann Christoph Arnold, *Why Forgive?* (Walden, NY: The Plough Publishing House, 2010), 184.
3. Arnold, *Why Forgive?*, 187.

Chapter 3: The Best Way to Forgive

1. Laura Hillenbrand, *Unbroken* (New York: Random House, 2010), 396–97.
2. Roy Lessin, "God Sent Us a Saviour," DaySpring Cards, https://www.dayspring.com/roy-lessin-god-sent-us-18-christmas-boxed-cards-kjv.
3. Martin Luther King Jr., http://www.thekingcenter.org/blog/mlk-quote-week-sticking-love.
4. Julie Barnhill, *Radical Forgiveness* (Carol Stream, IL: Tyndale, 2004), 164.
5. Stephen R. Covey, *The 7 Habits of Highly Effective People: Powerful Lessons in Personal Change* (New York: Simon & Schuster, 2013).
6. R. A. Wise, ed., *Wise Quotes of Wisdom* (Bloomington, IN: AuthorHouse, 2011), 106.
7. Robert D. Enright, *Forgiveness Is a Choice* (Washington, D.C.: American Psychological Association, 2001). For more information, see Amelia R. Farquhar, "The Healing Power of Forgiveness," Redbook, November 17, 2008, http://www.redbookmag.com/body/mental-health/a4336/emotional-healing-forgiveness/ and Dean Robbins, "Forgiveness Expert Robert Enright Reveals the Keys to Emotional Healing," Continuing Studies, September 17, 2015, https://news.continuingstudies.wisc.edu/forgiveness-expert-robert-enright-reveals-the-keys-to-emotional-healing/.

Chapter 4: Count the Costs of Unforgiveness

1. Loren Toussaint et al., "Effects of Lifetime Stress Exposure on Mental and Physical Health in Young Adulthood: How Stress Degrades and Forgiveness Protects Health," *Journal of Health Psychology*, August 19, 2014, http://journals.sagepub.com/doi/abs/10.1177/1359105314544132. Also Alexandra Sifferlin, "Forgiving Other People Is Good for Your Health," *Time*, June 16, 2016, http://time.com/4370463/forgiveness-stress-health/.

2. "Forgiveness: Your Health Depends on It," John Hopkins Medicine, https:// www.hopkinsmedicine.org/health/healthy_aging/healthy_connections/ forgiveness-your-health-depends-on-it.
3. Razali Salleh Rohd, "Life Event, Stress and Illness," *The Malaysian Journal of Medical Sciences,* May 22, 2008, https://www.ncbi.nlm.nih.gov/pmc/articles/ PMC3341916/.
4. "The Effects of Stress on Your Body," WebMD, https://www.webmd.com/ balance/stress-management/effects-of-stress-on-your-body.
5. Josh McDowell, *Undaunted* (Carol Stream, IL: Tyndale Momentum, 2012).
6. https://vpge.stanford.edu/people/fred-luskin.
7. "Effects of Group Forgiveness Intervention on Perceived Stress, State and Trait, Anger, Symptoms of Stress, Self-Reported Health and Forgiveness (Stanford Forgiveness Project)," Forgive for Good, https://learningtoforgive.com/ research/effects-of-group-forgiveness-intervention-on-perceived-stress-state-and-trait-anger-symptoms-of-stress-self-reported-health-and-forgiveness-stanford-forgiveness-project/.
8. Thanks to https://www.wisdomtimes.com/blog/health-benefits-of-forgiveness/ for their help with this list.

Chapter 5: Show God Where It Hurts

1. "55 Surprising Divorce Statistics for Second Marriages," HealthResearchFunding .org, March 20, 2015, https://healthresearchfunding.org/55-surprising-divorce-statistics-second-marriages/.
2. Stepfamily Statistics, The Stepfamily Foundation, http://www.stepfamily.org/ stepfamily-statistics.html.
3. "Understanding child sexual abuse," American Psychological Association, December 2011, http://www.apa.org/pi/families/resources/child-sexual-abuse.aspx.
4. Peter Drucker, *Management,* revised edition (New York: Collins, 2008), 127.
5. Mahatma Gandhi, "Interview to the Press," Young India, March 26, 1931, *Collected Works of Mahatma Gandhi* Online Vol. 51, 301, http://www .gandhiashramsevagram.org/gandhi-literature/mahatma-gandhi-collected-works-volume-51.pdf.
6. Linda Hogan, *Solar Storms* (New York: Scribner, 1995), 5.
7. Haruki Murakami, *What I Talk about When I Talk about Running* (New York, Vintage International Publisher, 2009), vii.
8. Max Lucado, *Grace Happens Here* (Nashville: Thomas Nelson, 2012), 130–32.
9. Jonathan Lemire, "Victoria Ruvolo, Who Was Hit By Turkey Nearly 6 Years Ago, Forgives Teens for Terrible Prank," *New York Daily News,* November 7, 2010, http://www.nydailynews.com/new-york/victoria-ruvolo-hit-turkey-6-years-forgives-teens-terrible-prank-article-1.455256.
10. Vicky Ruvolo has also written a book about her experiences, titled *No Room for Vengeance.*

Chapter 6: Do You Want to Get Well?

1. Bill Hewitt and Tom Nugent, "Kevin Tunell Is Paying $1 a Week for a Death He Caused and Finding the Price Unexpectedly High," *People,* April 16, 1990, http://people.com/archive/kevin-tunell-is-paying-1-a-week-for-a-death-he-caused-and-finding-the-price-unexpectedly-high-vol-33-no-15/.

2. Lee Keath, "Iranian Woman Forgives Son's Killer at the Gallows," *Associated Press, San Diego Union Tribune*, April 17, 2014, http://www.sandiegounion tribune.com/sdut-iranian-woman-forgives-sons-killer-at-the-gallows-2014apr17-story.html.

Chapter 7: No Longer a Victim

1. See 2 Timothy 1:7.
2. Adam Selzer, "Tracking Down a Groucho Quote," November 6, 2014, http://adamselzer.blogspot.com/2014/11/tracking-down-groucho-quote.html.
3. Robert Anthony, *Beyond Positive Thinking* (Garden City, NY: Morgan James, 2007), 145.
4. "Amish School Shooting," https://lancasterpa.com/amish/amish-school-shooting/.

Chapter 8: Don't Lose Your Temper—Find It

1. Rose Arce, "From Anger to Forgiveness: Man Befriends Brother's Killer," CNN, April 13, 2013, http://religion.blogs.cnn.com/2013/04/13/from-anger-to-forgiveness-man-befriends-brothers-killer/comment-page-4/.
2. Theodore Dorpat, *Crimes of Punishment* (New York: Algora, 2007), 253.
3. Mothers Against Drunk Driving, https://www.madd.org/history/.
4. Cheri Carter-Scott, *If Love Is a Game, These Are the Rules* (New York: Broadway Books, 1999), 105.
5. Editors of Reader's Digest, *Quotable Quotes* (Pleasantville, NY: The Reader's Digest Association, 1997), 87.

Chapter 9: Remember How to Forget

1. James Ritchie, "Fact or Fiction?: Elephants Never Forget," Scientific American, January 12, 2009, https://www.scientificamerican.com/article/elephants-never-forget/.
2. Faith, Hope, & Psychology, "80% of Thoughts Are Negative . . . 95% Are Repetitive," *The Miracle Zone* (blog), February 18, 2013, https://faithhopeandpsychology.wordpress.com/2012/03/02/80-of-thoughts-are-negative-95-are-repetitive/.
3. Corrie ten Boom, "Guideposts Classics: Corrie ten Boom on Forgiveness," *Guideposts*, July 24, 2014, https://www.guideposts.org/better-living/positive-living/guideposts-classics-corrie-ten-boom-on-forgiveness.
4. Dr. Aaron Temkin Beck has served as a psychiatrist and a professor emeritus in the Department of Psychiatry at the University of Pennsylvania. More info at https://en.wikipedia.org/wiki/Aaron_T._Beck.
5. Amy Morin, "The Definition of Cognitive Reframing," *VeryWell Mind*, January 22, 2018, https://www.verywell.com/reframing-defined-2610419.
6. Amber Cassady, "Shooting Victim Chooses Forgiveness," *Baptist News Global*, July 25, 2012, https://baptistnews.com/article/shooting-victim-chooses-forgiveness/#.Wl5mjJM-eRs.
7. Dylan Stableford, "Colorado Shooting Victim on James Holmes: 'I Forgive Him with All My Heart,'" *The Lookout*, July 26, 2012, https://www.yahoo.com/news/blogs/lookout/colorado-shooting-victim-forgives-holmes-142413141.html.
8. "Aurora Faithful See Light in Dark Days," *The Sentinel*, August 2, 2012, https://www.sentinelcolorado.com/news/aurora-faithful-see-light-in-dark-days/.

Chapter 10: Restoring Broken Relationships

1. Mona Herold Vanni, Find a Grave, https://www.findagrave.com/memorial/ 30254761/mona-vanni.
2. Lane Palmer, "Paco . . . All Is Forgiven," *The Christian Post*, February 5, 2007, https://www.christianpost.com/news/paco-all-is-forgiven-25617/.
3. Julia Harriette Johnston, "Grace Greater than Our Sin," 1910, http://library .timelesstruths.org/music/Grace_Greater_than_Our_Sin/.

Chapter 11: Forgive Yourself and Make Peace with God

1. My translation.

Chapter 12: Your Fate Is Not Your Destiny

1. Brad Schmitt, "MercyMe's Bart Millard Thought His Father Was Going to Kill Him," *Tennessean*, February 13, 2018, https://www.tennessean.com/story/ entertainment/music/2018/02/13/bart-millard-mercyme-can-only-imagine-movie-book-father-abuse/320728002/.
2. Booker T. Washington, *Up from Slavery* (New York: Doubleday, Page & Co, 1901), 39.
3. For Joseph's full story, read Genesis 37, 39–45.
4. "Kintsugi: The Centuries-Old Art of Repairing Broken Pottery with Gold," My Modern Met, April 25, 2017, https://mymodernmet.com/kintsugi-kintsukuroi/.

Acknowledgments

First and foremost, I'd like to sincerely express my appreciation to you for picking up my book. Legendary writer Margaret Mitchell took ten years to write the classic *Gone with the Wind*. It took me about ten years to write my book, but that's where our similarities end! I only share this to assure you that this book is the product of years of intense study, practical ministry, and personal experience.

There are so many people who have enriched my life over the years, but there are a few who have impacted my life in the area of forgiveness more than any others.

Like many mature Christians, I thought I knew everything there was to know about forgiveness until I met David, Faith, and Larry from a small group called Provocation Ministries. They not only saved my marriage at a time of crisis, they taught me how to forgive my way to freedom. Without their loving patience, biblical instruction, and diligence, this book would have never been written.

As my passion for forgiveness grew, I was introduced to Dr. Dick Tibbits's *Forgive to Live* books, seminars, and resources. His amazing approach to forgiveness provided the teaching and discipline I needed for my passion. I will be forever grateful for his generous spirit to share all that God had taught him about forgiveness so this liberating message could be heard by as many people as possible.

Most of all, I want to acknowledge my best friend, Andy Lay, whom I dearly love. He has been my truest friend for more than forty years, and more than any man I know, he demonstrates the love of Jesus to me. Andy has been my confidant, counselor, mentor, and model of how to live a victorious Christian life. Some men light candles in the darkness. Andy Lay carries a torch that not only shines the love of God to the world but also leads the way for others to follow.

HOW TO BE A HERO WHEN YOU'RE FEELING ANYTHING BUT SUPER

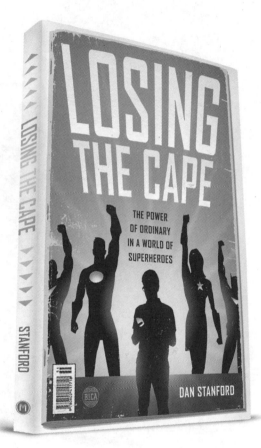

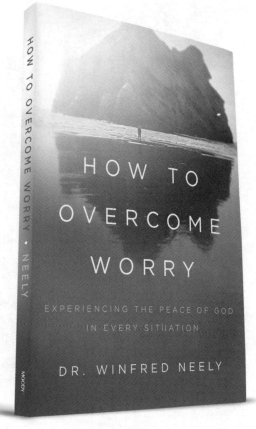

BECOMING A PERSON OF GODLY COURAGE IN A SINFUL WORLD

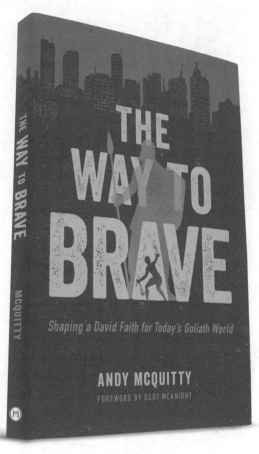

MOODY Publishers®

From the Word to Life®

The Way to Brave guides readers through the five ways God prepared David to be intrepid in facing the giant who opposed him. The qualities and experiences David possessed are the ones Christians need today. Pastor Andy McQuitty will walk you through what those are and how they can mark your life, bolstering you for the storms ahead.

978-0-8024-1807-4 | also available as an eBook

IT'S TIME TO GET YOUR LIFE BACK

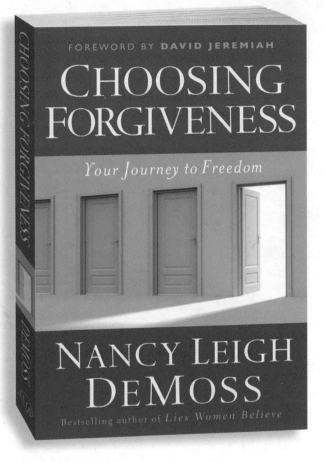